STRETCH MARKS

Essays for the Unfinished Woman

Joan Anderson

Also by Joan Anderson

A Year by the Sea
An Unfinished Marriage
A Walk on the Beach
A Weekend to Change Your Life
The Second Journey

STRETCH MARKS: Essays for the Unfinished Woman
Copyright © 2015 by Joan Anderson. All rights reserved.

www.joanandersononline.com

capewoman@msn.com

ISBN: 978-0-9859123-5-2

ISBN-13: 0985912359

1. Anderson, Joan. 2. Middle-aged women—United States—Psychology. 3. Middle-aged women—United States—Conduct of life. 4. Self-realization in women. 5. Aged women—Conduct of Life. 6. Anderson, Joan—Marriage. 7. Women—Massachusetts—Cape Cod—Biography. 8. Cape Cod, Mass.—Description and Travel.

Front cover art: "Block Island 1978" by Gretchen Dow Simpson used with permission and acknowledgement.

Cover design by Ann Moss

First Edition

DEDICATION

For all those who helped me stretch...

CONTENTS

AUTHOR'S NOTE

The Japanese place a great deal of value on chance meetings. Luckily I've had many, all of which have helped shape my continuous journey and sense of self, as well as my values, outlook, and purpose in life. There was an Ambassador's wife in Africa from whom I learned ordinary diplomacy. Oprah showed me how to give of myself sparingly. Arlene Alda urged me to never compare. A UPS man showed me the delight of presupposing another's need. A Scottish hotel keeper urged me to make amends sooner rather than later. And the theologian William Sloan Coffin taught me to know that I am enough. Beyond these specific personalities are the weekend retreaters and my readers—all unfinished, seeking women who have shared as much with me as I with them.

Some of those random connections stayed, becoming tent poles of my evolving existence. Mentioned many times in these essays is my mentor Joan Erikson, wife and collaborator of the famed psychotherapist Erik Erikson. She was the inspiration for my memoirs and a good friend. The other two women whose writings gave birth to my journey are Jungian therapist Clarissa Pinkola Estés, author of *Women Who Run With the Wolves,* and Florida Scott Maxwell, also a Jungian scholar. I introduce them here so I don't have to continue to identify them in the essays themselves.

There are many more women who have left a mark upon my soul, but the list itself would fill a book. Instead, know that their teachings are etched into mine and their support has given me the courage to write this collection of essays.

I am grateful for all of them.

Thank you, and enjoy.

STRETCH MARKS

In the movie *Shirley Valentine*, the heroine attempts to cover up her stretch marks as she's about to make love to her Greek suitor. True to Mediterranean fashion, the lover insists her imperfections are a badge of honor—remnants from the embracing and creation of life. Stretch marks should be celebrated, he tells her. Revered.

Shirley ran away to Greece intent on rebelling against domesticity, her dominating husband, and her grown, dependent children. She was determined to become a new Shirley, someone more attuned to that once-upon-a-time woman who'd gotten lost in life's mundane rituals.

Finally given permission to accept herself, she dives in with reckless abandon.

The Greek definition of "intention" is: *to stretch toward something*. In Shirley's case, she made a mad dash abroad in order to see herself anew, but we all have our own ways of stretching. For me, that's why I write—to reach toward a better understanding of who I am and what I believe, and then to evolve and change.

No doubt I've been marred along the way, tripping over my own feet as I stumble toward my next stage. But instead of getting rid of those resulting stretch marks, scars, and blemishes, I believe they should be shown off with pride. For the situations that created them served as life lessons, each one telling the story of when I worked through adversity to bring myself or others through a portal. With each mark comes progress, offering the experiences I've needed to make me who I am today and lay the foundation of who I'll become tomorrow.

Everything I know I've learned from living, not books. What's more, it's all come in fits and starts. Evolution is not linear nor are my thoughts. Surely I've airbrushed a few of my memories, and some thoughts and feelings have faded, but the important aspects of a woman's life— becoming an adult, the joy and failure of marriage, growing children, and incidental happenings—continue to be, for me, what's important.

These tales serve as a tribute to our resilience as women, and it's my hope that they engender discussion and soulful understanding in each of you. The agonies and ecstasies of my past are not peculiar to me, rather I am seeking to define woman like everyone else. As a general rule we tend to see things collectively and find companionship in our commonality. It often helps us to not feel alone, ashamed, or afraid when we discover that what we think or do others also think or do. Certainly open sharing can save us a trip to the therapist's office. Like Joan Erikson said, "If we don't share our feelings, we might as well be men."

So may you find solace in the thoughts herewith and celebrate all the marks you've created on your body and in your consciousness. Because each one means you've dared to live, to strive, and to stretch toward *something*.

Accepting the self

Since I am wholly unprepared
for what comes next in my life,
I am forced to content myself
with that which is before me.

1

Growing Up, Finally

S T R E T C H I N G

toward WISDOM

GROWING UP, FINALLY

Somewhere along my 70th year I finally woke up. Or had I finally grown-up? In any case, I'd been stuck in adolescence for as long as I could justify it, and I badly needed to move on.

Always avoiding the aging process altogether, I would look at snapshots of older relatives and vow it would never happen to me. I wasn't against aging, per se, it just wasn't my thing. Like my hero Peter Pan I've been stalling adulthood forever, leaning on others so as not to be the brave grown-up responsible for everyone else's happiness. Each birthday was a mere mark on the calendar that had nothing to do with getting older.

Deep inside, however, I harbored a self-inflicted anxiety so profound that I landed in a psychiatrist's office. Near the end of my second year of weekly appointments, I blurted out: "What *is* the matter with me?"

"Acute maladjustment to adult life," he answered glibly. "That's all."

I slumped in my chair. "That's the best you can come up with?" I gasped. "A little-known, benign disorder?"

Instead of relief I felt wounded. Having spent hundreds of hours, not to mention dollars, trying to find deliverance from my varying levels of neurosis, which included severe hypochondria and a fear of death, his pronouncement shamed me. I ducked out of the office.

Ever so gradually, realities began creeping into my consciousness that forced me to acknowledge my continuing evolution. My daily jog became a walk thanks to my diminished stamina; over-the-counter reading glasses no longer served my blurred vision; and phone calls from the drug store reminding me to pick up prescriptions were more frequent than calls from family and friends. On top of it all, a photo album I found chronicling me at every age and stage served as undeniable proof that most of my life was behind me. I hadn't just grown up. I'd grown old!

Then the unthinkable happened—the death of my parents. As we shoveled dirt into their graves the truth set in: the torch had been passed. There was no backup or safety net, no wise elder to whom I could turn. I was now the matriarch.

Further hammering this entelechy home was an attorney friend I ran into at a funeral. "We're in the front lines now," he quipped with a wink. It took a full minute for his dark humor to sink in, and by the time it had, I didn't feel like laughing.

Then again, if he could embrace aging with humor, why not I? I commissioned an artist to create a road sign I'd seen in Scotland of two stooped souls with canes in hand. It reads: Elderly Crossing. We put it in our driveway as a joke but also to remind ourselves that it was time to welcome the inevitable. As my husband says, the long sleep is coming sooner than we think, and as the sign relays, it's time to cross over. Enough indulging in self-afflicted anxiety when I know better. *To dwell in distress or look at things to bless,* so the saying goes.

All right, so I'm finally the elder. I've left Never Never Land for good and with it the lingering fear that aging means diminished power. Instead, to my pleasant surprise, I've learned that with each new year we actually have an opportunity to expand.

How astonishing, really. In the course of a life our bodies and minds travel through so many different phases until eventually—hopefully—a mature person emerges. Even if it takes 70 years.

Perhaps spending time in therapy with my fears and phobias wasn't indulgent after all. Life is a series of little births and deaths, endings and beginnings. In adolescence, we leave our childhood body and grow into another. We develop a unique personality and then enter a world beyond the familiar institutions that nurtured us. Finally, we become scholars of self and soul, working on our individualities until the end.

"As long as we are alive, we must keep transforming ourselves," said Joan Erikson. "I thought you plateaued somehow when you got older, but instead, you just keep truckin'." At 90, she came to see that we are all capable of new tricks.

Meanwhile, my friend Annie, who's 74 but looks 50, absolutely refuses to talk about age. "It matters not," she asserts, "and I don't want to be defined by something as silly as that."

I'm beginning to accept this odd stage, or whatever you want to call it, awakened to its options and aware there's no time to squander. Being the elder—which in other cultures denotes dignity, integrity, and power—is not so bad after all. While mentally and physically it's taken some getting used to, my well-honed instincts are driving me forward. There's a sense of liberation I didn't expect to feel, coupled with the freedom one gains when letting go of old ideas. I've finally faced the ticking clock and claimed my being. I know what I know. Something invisible and silent is pulling at me.

2

You Don't Get a Gold Watch for Menopause

S T R E T C H I N G

toward CHANGE

YOU DON'T GET A GOLD WATCH
FOR MENOPAUSE

A while ago, before the "change of life" was a reality I fully understood, I was sitting in my best friend's backyard ruminating about the prospect of our lives once our children had grown and gone. "We have to start making some decisions for ourselves," she said with a righteous tone in her voice. "After all, you don't get a gold watch for menopause."

Dissolving into hysterical laughter at the combined pithiness and poignancy of her statement, I concurred. Having lived halfway to a hundred in a fairly prescribed way—marriage, children, house in the suburbs, volunteering at the kid's school—I wasn't able to imagine life without its familiar parameters. But I surely didn't want to be dismissed just because my body retired from one of its most noble acts—the producing and feeding of children. Even though it'd yet to happen, I felt as if my very femininity was being called into question, and I hadn't the faintest idea what to do about it. All I knew was I wasn't about to up and quit.

My laughter died down, and we sat in shared silence.

"Who wants a gold watch anyway?" I finally insisted. "After so many years marching along to everyone else's schedule, a watch is the last thing I want. Frankly, I'd prefer to be off the clock and on vacation."

I couldn't begin to calculate the thousands of dinners cooked, errands run, doctor's appointments kept, or holiday celebrations produced. It felt as though we'd more than earned our stripes in the name of service to our families.

"To be honest," I added with a tip of my wine glass, "the 'pause' part of menopause is looking pretty inviting to me."

A decade later, I tip my glass back at the woman I was that day. Having come through to the other side, I've learned menopause is actually a chance for liberation. Culturally we focus on what menopause means in terms of a woman's body. It's a drying up. A time of newly emerging wrinkles, sagging flesh, blurred vision, and, horror of all horrors, a rounded belly. For those of us who crave the gold watch, an appointment with the plastic surgeon is the answer. As for me, I can't bear to engage in the perpetual upkeep of a fleeting (or long-gone) youth for the rest of my life. I'd rather work with nature and embrace change.

Life keeps moving, and as the years go by, I keep realizing I can't control its course; I can only adapt. Part of adapting has been learning to see things anew. We shouldn't feel used up and washed ashore just because our bodies have aged. If anything, we should be celebrating the women we have become.

Maybe the physical changes would be easier to accept if we honored the journey that preceded them. We mark graduations, marriage, birth, even death with fanfare. Why not menopause? What if we were to create a celebration that honored our "pause" and recognized our achievements—crises managed, lessons mastered, attitudes and assumptions reversed? If we chose to pay tribute to who we are today, perhaps we could be spared the depression that comes from longing for the way we were.

Joan Erikson always said, "Life is a progression. We are meant to be aware and eager to greet the next passage."

Though looking toward that next phase can sometimes be scary or daunting, I now tip my glass to the woman who's already journeyed through it. I know she's tipping her glass back at me from the other side, her wrist gold-watch free.

3

The Camera Never Blinks

S T R E T C H I N G

toward DNA

THE CAMERA NEVER BLINKS

My brother had just finished converting our father's home movies into a DVD when he invited me to partake in some "real living history." I accepted, fully expecting to witness the two of us growing up in staged vignettes a la *Father Knows Best*. No doubt my brother and I would be the leading characters in the family drama, but I was just as eager to see the supporting players.

Settling into an easy chair with a glass of wine, I prepared to be awash in nostalgia. There inevitably would be tears and laughter as I watched our parents produce birthday parties, family vacations, and Christmas year after year—all of us playing the ham as the camera closed in.

As the lights went out, the original Anderson family popped up on the flat-screen TV amidst a typical summer's day. My brother and I were splashing around in a tiny canvas pool with neighborhood playmates while grandpa repaired the back stoop and mom distributed popsicles. Our father was just beginning to perfect the craft of filmmaking with his tiny 8 mm camera, so he'd apparently chosen to experiment on a day when the stakes were low.

The adults looked exactly as I remembered—right down to my mother's curly, cropped hair, halter top, and shorts to show off her Betty Grable legs. But the children, even though they were we, seemed like strangers. I couldn't connect with that little blond girl on the screen who constantly pouted while her brother stole the show. You could tell she just wanted to be herself, not the well-behaved child they kept trying to cajole into staged snapshots and poses.

As the footage reeled on—and the movie began to resemble Norman Rockwell's *Saturday Evening Post* covers—it was clear my father fancied himself a Cecil B. DeMille. He never missed those significant moments befitting ordinary life. Most poignant was the wartime Christmas where old toys were repainted to look new, and we children awed in amazement at the tree and all the trimmings, a sight unveiled for the first time Christmas morning.

During the initial hour it was amusing to look back so vividly on our young lives. Astounding, too, was this reversed perception of our parents. They looked so adult, so together, and so in charge—utterly confident human beings exhibiting qualities that to this day I've yet to own.

By the second hour, however, I'd begun to recognize a fissure between the portrayal of our family life and the way I felt while living it. In many ways I wasn't witnessing life as it really was, but rather how our parents wanted our life to be perceived. I put down my wine and straightened up, paying close attention to body language, expressions, and real or fabricated joy.

I tried to remain neutral as each segment played out, intent on looking for authenticity. What I was shocked to discover was how much my formative years wavered through different personas, each an attempt to be what I thought I needed to be in order to gain acceptance in one of the 17 towns we called home.

Going to the movies every Saturday gave me plenty of material to work with, and it was there I discovered what I thought I wanted in life. For the admission price of 12 cents, I became part of Mario Lanza's world in *The Great Caruso* or Gene Kelly's saga in *Singing in the Rain*. Needless to say, I was a hopeless romantic.

Perhaps in his own way my sensitive father shared my imagination, and we both struggled to accept that our life at home wasn't as glamorous as those depicted by Hollywood or as ideal as a Normal Rockwell painting. In reality, we were no different from any other middle-class family at the time. Or were we?

As other relatives appeared and disappeared from the screen, I chuckled at the diversity and the dysfunction. Ours was an eclectic group composed of obsessive compulsives, hypochondriacs, narcissists, passive-aggressive types, and alcoholics. Some refused to perform and would cover the camera lens with their hands, while others were so self-conscious that they sat with frozen smiles plastered across their faces. Yet even within those moments of feigned perfection, their true personalities shone through, and despite their flaws, each character was a survivor—all of them hard-working, resilient people, not the WASPish clan my father was trying to portray.

If one is lucky, illusions will find a way of dissipating as life is lived. So it happened on this particular afternoon when I awakened to yet another truth: who I am today is very much built on the raw material of my relatives.

One grandmother was overly opinionated while the other was stubborn and stoic. One grandpa had a violent temper while the other was meek and mild. And I never noticed how particular, detailed-oriented, and very much in control, like me, my mother had been.

But it was in two of my aunts that I saw the biggest glimmer of myself. Named after each of them, I seem to have taken on their unique and very different brands. My father never could get a stationary shot of my Aunt Elsie, whose every move was dramatic and intense. She would fling her arms as she told tales of faraway places, sipping wine with every downstroke and laughing at herself, knowing everyone deemed her eccentric.

My Aunt Punch preferred to hold court, always sitting like a queen at the head of the table. She was content to do nothing more than keep the conversation going at a high level and relish the wild debates that followed.

Both, along with all the women in the film, very subtly sought control, never wanting to follow the rules of others. While it made for a messy kitchen, it seemed the matriarchy was alive and well in our family. Each was addicted to perfection, for sure, and they all strove to be individuals.

It was clear that I'd become a carbon copy of women who refused to be carbon copies, stuck with certain attributes gifted to me by default.

Joan Erikson believed we arrive into this world with genetic traits formed in utero, and we're not to ignore them but use them. "Some things you just can't change," she would say. "They are indelibly printed on your soul. You've no choice but to go with it—use these strengths and build on them."

As I continued to watch this unritualized documentation of my past, I began traveling toward some distant maturity. If I hadn't felt like a full-fledged grown-up at the beginning of the afternoon, I was now. My elders had shown me how they thought life should be lived, and I had become a weaving of all of them put together. Even with a few traits I'd rather not have inherited, I feel a certain sense of security knowing there's a long line of ancestors standing behind me.

As such, I shall take what I've garnered from each one and add in my own color. For as the poet David Whyte wrote:

We lived in the place as we were meant to
And then surprised by our abilities
Became the ancestor of it all.

4

Figure Faults

S T R E T C H I N G

toward SELF-RESPECT

FIGURE FAULTS

We're coming up on that dreadful time of year again. Not that I don't like spring or summer, but warm weather means less clothing and more exposure—the kind a maturing body like mine would just as soon do without. Still, living on Cape Cod and going to the beach every day means donning a bathing suit, so for once I vowed to get a jumpstart on my appearance. Come March, I hired a personal trainer and joined a gym.

We got right in, tackling my aching back, sagging arms, and overall physique. Within a month I'd actually lost several inches in various parts of my aging body, but there, in the middle, remained an ugly kangaroo pouch I no longer could suck in.

Short of liposuction I was doomed, not to mention embarrassed. I couldn't drape shawls and wear layers in the heat! One last option remained—*Redbook's* Tummy Makeover. By doing just six exercises three times a week for 12 weeks, I was guaranteed to lose two tummy inches at the very least. I was faithful to this regimen—honest I was—but when I gazed at my profile in our full-length mirror there'd been zero change. Pissed, I tossed the magazine into the trash. There should have been a disclaimer.

Now desperate, I dove into the Lands' End catalog certain to find a suit to complement my curve-less figure. Sure enough, there were numerous options, all promising to flatter every shape, boost confidence, and make anyone look a size smaller. I settled on three choices, each claiming tummy control and other figure flaw-disguising tricks. Eureka! There was hope, even for me.

When the Fed Ex package arrived on my doorstep two days later, I was eager to try on my purchases and put this arduous task behind me. I chose the Swim Dress first, as it appeared to be the most forgiving. But as I struggled to tug on the Spandex and tuck my rolls into place, my excitement quickly dulled. One quick glance in the mirror told me this suit would be going back. I resembled my grandmother at a Coney Island beach back in 1930. Hardly the image I wanted to put forth.

Not to worry, I encouraged myself. *I have two other styles to try*. But after prying on the black-and-white Slimming Suit my hopes drooped like the boobs I was trying to perk up. The wide band of shirring, which was supposed to shrink my middle, caused my tummy to protrude all the more.

With my "last chance suit" waiting in the box, I prayed the Slender Tulip would be just right. Once I finally figured out how the darn thing was supposed to hang, I stood back and looked at my demoralized reflection. The draped overlay meant to minimize the hips only made my camouflage attempts all the more obvious.

I felt hopeless, not to mention infuriated by the humor my husband was finding in the situation. As he watched me peel off the last suit, he even suggested I was having a hysterical pregnancy!

"There's always the maternity store," a friend suggested the next day. "I've been reduced to going there for pull-on slacks and shorts when I've gained a few extra pounds."

"You've got to be kidding," I snapped. But with time running out I had little choice. Deflated, I headed to the mall—a place I rarely visit—and ducked into A Pea in the Pod hoping no one would see me.

"I'm trying to find a bathing suit for my pregnant daughter-in-law," I lie to the clerk. "We're going on a cruise and she lives in Alaska. No way can she find one there."

Internet shopping hadn't crossed my mind.

"They're in the back of the store," she answered, eyeing me in a way that immediately told me she knew. Even so, it felt better to mutter some sort of explanation before trotting to the rack and sifting through the possibilities.

As the hangers scraped against the bar—no, no, no, no—it occurred to me that shame is an awful emotion. Why can't I just be bold and bawdy like the lady who wrote *When I Am An Old Woman I Shall Wear*

Purple? But no. I had pride and, unfortunately, standards. The swimwear was hideous.

I was about to cut my losses and escape when the clerk pointed out some tennis dresses made with Spandex and nylon that might just work. "I wear them myself on hot summer days," she confessed with a sympathetic smile. "You'd be surprised how many women come in here just because they want to be comfortable."

Oh God, I thought, *she really does know!*

I grabbed an Adidas outfit, slapped my credit card on the counter, and counted the seconds until the sale was complete. Mission accomplished, I raced for the door holding tight to a swimsuit I'd not yet tried on but one I was determined to wear for years to come.

On the way home I passed a tennis club, and for a split second I imagined what I would look like sashaying across the court in the very attire I'd just purchased. Then it dawned on me: it didn't matter what I wore, I'd probably never play tennis again seeing as though speed and agility were adjectives of my past.

I was about to slip further into the depths of self-pity when I remembered a recent skiing vacation with my grandkids. Even though I couldn't keep up with them, I never once felt left behind—I was in the game, not standing on the sidelines taking pictures! Sharing a lift ride with a complete stranger, I'd even felt smug when he said, "I wish my mother was in the shape you're in and could do this kind of stuff with our kids."

Why did I keep longing for the body I had 20 years ago when I should be grateful for a body that allows me such freedom? Suddenly the angst caused by my bathing suit search seemed silly. We talk about coming of age, but part of me lagged behind. We're each made up of spirit, mind, *and* body. If I can't accept how my body is evolving, I will never be completely at peace with myself.

It was Clarissa Pinkola Estés who suggested, "most of us see our bodies as our undoing even though they protect, support, and fire our spirits." I now require this vessel to serve me in new ways. It's no longer an issue of fat versus figure or size versus sex appeal. It's about function, because I want, indeed *need*, to participate in my own life.

How soon I'd forgotten the joy of climbing in and out of the Grand Canyon, hiking the Inca Trail, or clocking hundreds of miles on the Cape Cod bike path. Even the exhilaration of flying down the hills behind my grandkids had been fleeting.

"Nothing tastes as good as thin feels," a skinny friend said as she ran by me on the jogging trail the other day. I watched her firm little fanny bounce down the tarmac and struggled to catch up. But then I stopped. I don't need to catch up...nor tighten up, perk up, or shape up for that matter. I'm ready to celebrate sustainability by maintaining a body that works—figure faults and all.

5

Time to Clean Out the Closet

STRETCHING

toward AUTHENTICITY

TIME TO CLEAN OUT THE CLOSET

It occurred to me while cleaning out my closet the other day that I should get rid of most everything. It wasn't that my clothes no longer fit—although some were a tad tight—rather they had more than outlived their usefulness. Hanging inside a handful of garment bags, for example, were three St. John suits, several sparkly cocktail outfits, and a Diane Von Furstenberg jersey wrap. Beneath them all sat an unopened bag of panty hose and eight pairs of heels.

This was the wardrobe of a public person, not a cloistered writer who lives by the sea. If truth be told, I need nothing more than jeans, sweaters, Birkenstocks, and, for that rare occasion, an Eileen Fisher ensemble. Keeping the other stuff felt like clinging to a past.

I began stripping the hangers, imagining myself a character in the C.S. Lewis fantasy *The Lion, the Witch, and the Wardrobe*. "One opens the door of a wardrobe," he writes, "and pushing past the coats becomes lost in a darkened forest from which one emerges after many adventures." Holding up a glimmering black dress, I was transported to a party celebrating my husband's retirement. The suit worn to meet my agent for the first time conjured memories of the book signings that followed. It'd been a heady decade, for sure, with me running fast and playing multiple roles. I became a grandmother, cared for and adored an aging mother, acclimated to a semi-retired husband, embraced an unexpected writing career, and enlarged my circle of very unfinished women.

As the garments piled like leaves on the floor, I grew more and more grateful for having come through so much—and for having shed so many layers along the way. More than clothes these had been costumes, masking my true style with what I believed I needed to portray.

The turning point came when a woman approached me before a book signing. "I pictured you in jeans and a yellow slicker," she said, obviously disappointed that I didn't personify the fisherwoman she thought I had become. She left me standing in my pant suit before I could even answer or give my speech. So much for dressing the role. *But no more*, I pronounced while tossing that pant suit aside. *Let my untidy life and self emerge!*

There comes a time to give up the façade. When Joan Erikson became a faculty wife at Harvard and was invited to tea, every woman in the room looked alike—tweed suits, silk blouses, stacked heels, and pearls. The next day she fled for a hippie store in downtown Cambridge and bought several pairs of tights and Putumayo smocks, vowing never again to appear in a tweed suit. She may have been Erik Erikson's wife, but she held fiercely to her own identity. Finally, I was learning to embrace mine.

Even so, a bittersweet poignancy hit me as I looked at my half-empty closet. So much was over, outlived, changed. The publishing world had become precarious and electronic, and navigating its murky waters had become strange and difficult. Although it was a blessing for my mother to be relieved of her suffering, it was still hard to let her go. The grandchildren, who once were mesmerized by my magic, were quickly growing up and moving on in their own worlds.

After a brief moment of mourning, I acquiesced. My simple task had symbolized the cleaning out of an old life to make room for a new one. I had no desire for another wardrobe or a more chaotic life. Nor did I wish to relive the experiences or lessons the last decade had provided. Instead, the space in my closet was urging me to make more space for me.

I stuffed my outdated wardrobe into garbage bags and headed off to a nearby thrift shop feeling refreshed and open to possibilities. Suddenly I was free again to explore the unknown future—and dress it as I saw fit.

6

Rebel With
a Cause

S T R E T C H I N G
toward LIBERATION

REBEL WITH A CAUSE

It's in my nature to defy convention. I eat ice cream with a fork, wear white whenever I please, and ignore Do Not Enter signs. Tell me how it's done, and I'll most certainly choose another path.

My taste for such behavior dates back to my formative years, when my outrageous Aunt Elsie held court at our family functions. Blonde and beautiful, her engaging tales and captivating twinkle sent my imagination into overdrive. She'd formed a common-law marriage with an exotic lover, birthed a child out of wedlock, traveled the world, and forever dripped in jewels and mink. For days after her visits I would pretend to gaze at the Eiffel Tower from my pied-à-terre, sipping champagne while regaling admirers with my charm. Everything about her was far more entertaining than my plain Aunt Mary, who paled in comparison.

My mother, on the other hand, preferred to wax poetic about Aunt Mary, whose honorable virtues were matched only by her exceptional conventionality. She stayed legally and religiously married to an extremely dull man for 50 years, brought up four very accomplished children, and never raised her voice. According to my mother's description, Aunt Mary loved domesticity more than anything else on the planet. And by my estimation, that was way more than any woman in her right mind should.

When my uncle recently compared me to Elsie I was flattered, but I knew deep down he didn't intend it as a compliment. Along with my mother, he believed women were meant to behave like Mary—a poster child for feminine repression. Elsie was the family's black sheep, and I was following in her footsteps. Running away from home, living apart from my husband for more than a year, and turning my adventures into a book was no way to accrue points in a respectable family, he'd said. Despite my distain, I'd felt stung by his comment. Living up to my own secret standards hadn't eliminated the disappointment of falling short of someone else's. So what's a rebel to do?

The pull to conform and meet everyone else's demands is strong, which is why it's important to get far enough away from their loud voices that they fade away, leaving only yours in their stead.

Clarissa Pinkola Estés insists women are wild by nature. The frustration so many of us feel comes from being tamed by a culture that spoon-feeds us values rather than encourages us to explore our own lives and express contradictions. Estés insists that to tame a woman is to cut her off from her instincts and intuitions—important traits for the feral feminine spirit.

"A healthy woman is like a wolf." she wrote. "She must be free to move, to speak, to be angry, and to create, as her soul needs to be frequently replenished."

I found one such tamed woman at my door on a cold winter's day. After reading *A Year By The Sea*, she was compelled to speak with me. Running away from her home in Vermont, she left behind her minister husband and their four children, all under six. A patronizing man, he constantly belittled the way she handled the household and the children. After years of such treatment, she'd come to believe she was the neurotic invalid he'd made her out to be. She hoped that since I'd done the same thing, I might affirm her actions.

We sat by the fireplace sipping cups of tea and talking for hours, her confusion and guilt slowly beginning to dissolve. Just as I thought we were getting somewhere she blurted out, "My husband says I'm selfish."

"Selfish!" I howled. "Up until now it appears you have been selfless, which is why you find yourself on empty!"

If it's in a woman's nature to nurture, then we must nourish ourselves. Unfortunately, no one else is pushing us toward a time out. We have to train ourselves to pause— not an easy trick in this world where women DO more than just BE.

"For once you listened to your heart," I insisted, "and removed yourself from the fire."

She left that night with a new sparkle in her eyes.

The habit of deference can grow like a cancer on the soul of a woman until what she becomes is out of her hands. Yet so many women can't ever seem to say no. Like my visitor, they see time away as selfish. Or worse, they fear being tagged as one of those feminists who burns bras and makes waves to stir up tension in the home.

When my book first came out I was labeled by the media as *the woman who got away, the runaway wife, the woman who took a vacation from marriage*—all meant to characterize me as self-serving. And they were right. But I wasn't hurting anyone in the process. I like to think that instead of being selfish I was being self-full, filling up my very spirit.

Primitive tribes have known the benefits of a time off for centuries. Women are sent away eight times a year to a quiet place where they tend only to themselves. The tribal fathers honor women's instincts and intuitions, knowing that by being off duty a woman can tap into these qualities and return home refreshed—with even more to contribute to family and community.

In America we get Mother's Day, and even having that day off is not always guaranteed!

"Every man has his own destiny," said writer Henry Miller. "The only imperative is to follow it, to accept it, no matter where it leads him."

Surely fellow writer Anna Quindlen echoed his sentiments when she gave a college commencement address to several hundred women. "The thing that is really hard and really amazing," she relayed, "is giving up on being perfect and beginning the work of becoming yourself."

I say its time to step out of line. Break a few rules. Make some unpopular choices. Why were we created as individuals if we're to behave like everyone else? Start now to act on your own behalf and sponsor yourself. Become powerful in your own right in your own life. And above all, never, never be tamed.

Esteeming the
Self

S   T   R   E   T   C   H   I   N   G

toward AFFIRMATION

ESTEEMING THE SELF

A few friends and I were readying our homes and lives for the onslaught of summer visitors when we made time in our busy schedules to get together. We already needed emotional support.

With adult children and their progeny about to descend, preparing our emotional selves was paramount. There were the various family dynamics we'd be sure to face: sibling rivalry, in-law competition, and yet-to-be-known tensions that hinted at underlying disquietude. Then there were the tiring tasks of feeding, clean up after, and managing guests. For me, there also existed the pressure to orchestrate exciting events and elaborate feasts.

Why did I assume it was my responsibility to create the magic and make these reunions run smoothly? Must I always go over the top?

After I uttered such sentiments aloud, the hostess offered her thoughts. "I rarely get involved in their agenda when they are here," she relayed. "But you, Joan… you fall into the overachiever category."

Great laughter rounded the table as I sat in shocked silence. As far as I was concerned, overachievers were Type A perfectionists with a need to control everything. And while they were successful with their premeditated agendas, they certainly weren't the most endearing personalities.

As the chuckles faded, one glaring realization stood in their wake: that was me to a T. My own son hinted at this during a previous visit. "Grammy is never quite satisfied with how things turn out," he'd told his boys with a tinge of sarcasm. "Her expectations are always too high."

Ouch.

When a comment stings, it usually means it's true. And being found out as certifiably OA was just plain humiliating.

But, my inner self contested, *I'm not alone!*

I looked around the table and realized everyone there could qualify as an overachiever, including the hostess herself. She'd set a color-coordinated table of fine china and fresh flowers, all for an impromptu lunch. Then there was Susie, who'd just finished bragging about the "Welcome to Cape Cod" basket she'd left at her step-children's cottage, stuffed to the brim with beach toys, guidebooks, fishing rods, tackle boxes, and even the makings for s'mores.

Mary was kicking off her family's reunion by renting a lighthouse for what she said would be a memorable start to their vacation, which also included tickets to a Red Sox game and a Fourth of July lobster bake on the beach. And even though Jane was having no family this year, the "time off" was allowing her to chair the church fair, host a baby shower, and amp up her Meals on Wheels volunteer work.

Could these women not see overachievement plastered all over their foreheads? Bewildered and irate, I left for home.

A few days later my phone rang. "I've been feeling very guilty ever since the luncheon," the hostess confessed, "singling you out as an overachiever."

"No problem," I answered. "My only complaint is that everyone there is an overachiever, don't you think?"

After a brief pause, she agreed. "I think it has to do with our lack of self-esteem," she suggested. "As we get old and are put out to pasture, socially and as parents, we have fewer and fewer chances to accrue feathers in our caps. We try even harder to be noticed and to make a difference. It's a vicious cycle, if you ask me. I'm just envious you can still try so hard."

Her statement got me thinking. Most women are bred to be helpers and caretakers—our sense of selves aligned to how well we can provide. *Better to give than to receive*, my mother would recite ad nauseam. To ensure the family noticed her labor-intensive existence, she'd also repeat the old adage: *A woman's work is never done*. Even in silence her message came across loud and clear;

she'd painted her motto on the kitchen wall in every house we'd ever lived. Another axiom she'd recant came from her childhood church: *We seek the best.*

Her daily mantra of service was expected to be my lot in life, too. I was, after all, *her* progeny. Falling short of her standards was akin to lowering the expectations I had for myself—and thereby belittling her mothering skills.

Perhaps through attrition her words rubbed off and sank in. In many ways, I do seek the best. One of my high school teachers claimed, "The minute you do more than is expected of you, you free yourself." At first I didn't understand, then she explained. "When you do, you're no longer limited by the minimum effort required." Her sentiment stuck, and I've since found going the extra mile to be self-satisfying in the end—even if tiring.

Maybe that's why I try so hard...for me. It's not about competing with my friends or colleagues, nor is it about exceeding my husband's or children's expectations. It's about deciding exactly how and where I want to make my mark. I once thought the only root to self-esteem was becoming rich or famous, thin and elegant, an accomplished scholar, or marrying up. Self-esteem means appreciating the self—recognizing my individual qualities and being fully aware of my gifts so as to use them.

The philosopher John O'Donohue once said, "However dull or ineffectual one may feel, something eternal is happening." We each are needed for what we bring to the world. And from family visits to time with friends, we're provided opportunities to fulfill our unique callings. The trick is to do so with a smile, for as Thomas Jefferson said, "Nothing is troublesome that we do willingly." For sure, learning to be my own woman is a lifetime's work.

8

Multitasking
No More

S T R E T C H I N G

toward PRESENCE

MULTITASKING NO MORE

It's fall, my favorite season. The weather has moved from muggy to brisk, and a New Year's feeling imbibes me as I organize my calendar to make room for fresh ventures. But this time I'm changing gears. I'm becoming more deliberate in my scheduling to ensure multitasking is a thing of the past.

This change of attitude occurred after a recent trip to Rockford, Illinois. I received an invitation to speak at a large women's group and jumped at the chance, because it meant I could visit two of my grandsons. Then, before I knew it, I'd squeezed in a speech at Harvard and lunch with a friend, all before my flight. After a late arrival, I headed straight to the guest room to work on my address. The next morning I made a brief visit to the boys' school, gave the speech to 300, and was so tired by the end of the day that I had to call it an early night. Before I could blink, I was on my way back to Cape Cod.

I returned home exhausted and tense, but, most of all, I was disappointed at how I'd rushed through so many moments. I'd been there in body but not in spirit, always preparing for the next event. Subsequently, I felt cheated and ashamed for trying so hard and receiving so little emotional currency in return. Not to mention the fact that I'd given a mediocre speech.

Many women strive to "be all things to all people" in order to serve as the great healer to those around them. According to Clarissa Pinkola Estés, this effort is not only draining but destructive to the psyche, "for a woman to attempt to enact an archetype is doing the impossible." Still, many of us (myself included) keep piling on the good deeds.

I chuckle every time I look at the mug that holds my pens. On it a woman sits at a cluttered desk—file drawer open, trashcan overflowing—talking on a phone propped awkwardly on her shoulder while typing hastily into a computer. Emblazoned underneath are the words: *Please, I can only do 17 things at a time.*

Well, no longer. Although once typical for me, wearing five or six hats appears to be impossible. I've concluded I can do only one thing at a time to do it well.

Busy is one thing, but being truly involved is entirely different. The latter, according to the dictionary, means really engaging, participating with others, and having an emotional connection. Being busy, on the other hand, is just that—trying to accomplish too much, too fast while missing out on meaningful experiences in the process.

The difference, I think, is focus. Perhaps that's why I put off returning a phone call to a significant friend until I have at least a half hour to spend on a real conversation. Or why I clear several hours to construct a scrapbook after a visit with my grandchildren, pouring over pictures and placing them in story form.

To accomplish anything of worth we need to slow down and concentrate. Isn't that what creative persons do? An artist to paint, a writer to collect her thoughts, a musician to compose, a saint to pray...and, yes, even a grandmother to remember.

In the end it's a matter of sponsoring myself. No one else is going to push me to make the choices only I know will work for me. Nor will anyone urge me to take my time at my pace.

I must learn moderation in order to savor each experience and step back whenever I sense I'm spreading myself too thin. It's like becoming my own personal coach, monitoring when I've hit the limit or when I can go a bit farther, all the while registering the moment.

The last couple of weeks I've taken to dancing around the house and singing my own version of *Groovy*: *Slow down, you move too fast...you want to make the moment last.* Thank you for the tune, Simon and Garfunkel. It's working miracles.

Embracing
relationships

Love needs space around it
in order to grow.

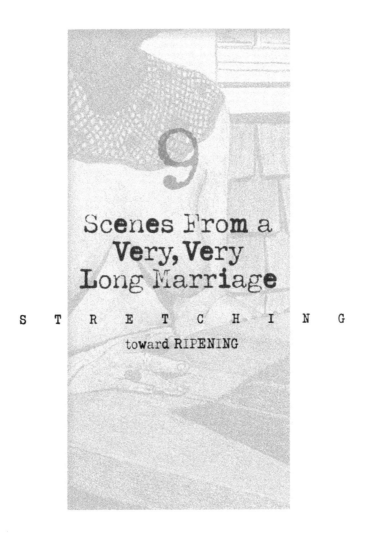

9

Scenes From a
Very, Very
Long Marriage

S T R E T C H I N G

toward RIPENING

SCENES FROM A VERY, VERY LONG MARRIAGE

It's hard to fathom I've been married for two thirds of my life. This December it will be 46 years, or 15,520 days to be exact. Because of my conjugal longevity I often feel like an endangered species, if not an already extinct one. Very few couples we know have been married to the same person for this long; in most cases they're on spouse number two or three.

Then there are those who just prefer to date. At first their conversations are peppered with sexual innuendo as they glance longingly at each other like lovesick puppies, experiencing feelings that have eluded me for quite some time. But even *their* fervor cools to a mild heat after six months or so. Wedded, or unwedded, bliss—a description no doubt coined by Hallmark—is a fantasy for sure.

My friend Judy claims it's utterly impossible to stay in love with anyone who shares your bathroom. In any case, she admits her version of bliss lasted for five or six years, followed by semi-miserable for four years, tolerable for 10, and mildly content for the rest of the time. She's now on her third husband, and from her unique vantage point it could be concluded that staying even happily married is easier said than done.

"No one knows why one couple makes it and another doesn't," Joan Erikson once told me. "Love is as fickle as snow. You can't make it happen or control how long it lasts."

I sense my husband and I stayed married simply because we're both strong-willed and stubborn. If we hadn't been in the Peace Corps and gotten married in East Africa, we never would have made it. Living such a raw existence with only each other to lean on created interdependency. It was a luxury, really, to live without influence or accouterments, as we were able to establish our own values and traditions. By comparison, many of today's duos start out with a plethora of wedding gifts, furniture, and the interference of elders. They barely have a chance to carve out their own niche.

We recently trotted off to Vermont for the wedding of a friend's daughter, where we were able to get an up-close-and-personal view of modern newlyweds. We stayed at one of those dreadful B&Bs where you're required to sit with strangers at a communal breakfast table and make small talk before you've even had a cup of coffee. Looking around at the mostly middle-aged couples I deduced—and they confirmed—that we were all there to attend weddings. The reporter in me couldn't resist asking point blank if any of them thought the marriages would last.

After a few uncomfortable coughs and a long pause, one brave wife said, judging by the body language at the previous night's rehearsal dinner, the socio-economic gap between the bride's and groom's families would work against them. Another mentioned their groom was unemployed—not an auspicious beginning. Still another relayed how the in-laws already had experienced a falling out, and there now seemed to be tremendous competition for the affections of their soon-to-be wedded children.

"It's all such a crapshoot," one woman piped up, her eyes darting toward her crimson-faced husband. "Anyone in their right mind knows it's a roll of the dice. These kids have no idea. It'll be culture shock tomorrow as they go from living a life for themselves to living it for another."

Come to think of it, we don't ever really know what we're in for until we've lived with a person for a while and their personality traits begin to surface. For us, it was my husband's pessimism that bubbled up and surprised me. He constantly sees his glass half empty. Every suggestion causes him to analyze the downside so thoroughly that our sons gave him the nickname Eeyore, the melancholy donkey in *Winnie the Pooh*. In his world everything looks black and white, while I prefer to see in Technicolor. He tends to be remote, while I share my issues with anyone willing to listen.

Imagine Eeyore and Tigger cohabiting, hardly speaking the same language and going about life with totally different objectives. It's a veritable attitudinal duel that we endure. Yet just as humor exists within the characters' commingling in *Winnie the Pooh*, so it endures in our crazy partnership. I suppose opposites attract. Perhaps two Tiggers competing for jumping space would be just as detrimental as two Eeyores holding everyone back.

Differences aside, our marriage always felt healthy as long as there were goals to achieve and no endings in sight. The babies were born, the first house was bought, and there were baseball, soccer, and lacrosse games to attend. Add graduations, school plays, and family vacations to the mix, and my husband and I hardly noticed we weren't *becoming* much together at all. Then came college, a string of girlfriends, and, finally, wives and grandchildren. Suddenly there were no more goals ahead. Our singular life had been lived.

Over time the various scenes blur...what we set out for in the beginning changed to something else...what once seemed disastrous became a silly memory later on. But alas, the ties that bound us together—homemaking, career building, and children—eventually unraveled, and we needed to let go of the future we thought had been prescribed to us. In its place came a mid-life malaise, further creased by economic setbacks, a job crisis, and invalid parents. When there wasn't drama, the daily calm fed into our agitation. Everything became too ordinary, and yet we were too weary to spice it up.

Then came the really bad patches. Arguments and disagreements grew frequent, and we seemed to take pleasure in slinging the unspoken, unpleasant truths we'd been holding onto for years. We considered divorce, endured a trial separation, and experienced our share of trysts and crushes. I tried to sweep the worst of our sins under the rug, but when that didn't assuage my guilt, I soothed my soul with comments credited to Robert Frost regarding forgiveness. He said he hoped his behavior would, in the end, be all right for what it was and that he could forgive himself for mistakes made by the person he had to be.

When my husband and I returned to the States some 40 years ago, we continued to need each other because we felt like strangers in our own land. We'd also learned that self-sufficiency is a delusion; a person needs a team or a partnership to survive. What the following years helped reveal is the difference between self-sufficiency and self-cultivation.

I came to recognize the rubs in our marriage occurred because of an inability to accept each other's personality quirks, willfulness, shortcomings, and egos. Fortunately, in the process of struggle and separation we were able to survive each other's growth spurts in order to come back together more matured.

Critiquing a marriage is like putting together a puzzle. All the pieces are spread out before you. The large ones represent significant moments, great disappointments, derailments, betrayals, new directions, additions, and celebrations—the highs and lows of a life. Also scattered about are the small, incidental pieces that form the border and everything in between. They are the "littles" that represent simple yet real moments that happen all the time, day after day, until they pile up to become the glue that holds it all together. These moments, along with one's history, helps bring the meaning of marriage to light.

I now see a good marriage as liberating. Love wants the most and the best for the beloved. That means time together, as well as time to explore independently and return with the jewels. At this stage of the game it might even be better to act a little divorced, releasing the rules we've upheld and the albatrosses we've placed upon each other's souls.

Perhaps we could have been spared some of the heartache along the way if we'd subscribed to the idea that marriage should come with a renewable contract. Periodically sitting down and talking frankly about how we were doing and what was and wasn't working might have softened our hearts a bit.

Even still, being a pathological altruist I always sensed we would create a happy ending somehow. When my husband gave me a Simon Pierce bowl for our 40th anniversary with the inscription *Married and Unfinished*, he had me all over again. Since then, our marriage has developed a new energy in which we are conscious of protecting the relationship against all odds. Moreover, we applaud the wholeness of the other while chuckling at the known quirks that have become our personal secrets. Our empowered friendship, in turn, has created a gentle intensity—no longer a roaring fire but warm coals glistening on the floor of the hearth.

Just tasting the sweetness of life is enough. If we had ever thought of untying the knot, it no longer is an option.

10

What's Sex Got to Do With It?

S T R E T C H I N G

toward INTIMACY

WHAT'S SEX GOT TO DO WITH IT?

There's no question: sex sells. This truism was evidenced by the line of people outside our local movie theatre, all anxious to see the new Meryl Streep and Tommy Lee Jones film *Hope Springs*. Billed as a love comedy about a middle-aged couple who had lost their spark, it seemed to bring hundreds to the theatre in hopes of finding their own lost sparks.

The subject of sex has always baffled me, so I joined the herd out of curiosity. Though, I admit, seeing a reflection of my marriage on screen caused me to squirm in my seat more than a few times. The stark reality of these two characters, who after 32 years of marriage were living in a now-atrophied relationship, rendered me nauseous. It actually hurt to watch Meryl primping in the bathroom mirror, dressed in a lovely blue negligee (mine's black) in hopes of seducing her husband. When he finally looked up from his golf magazine, puzzled as to why she was standing beside the bed smiling, I all but left the theatre.

One thing I can't stand or won't tolerate is someone growing remote, either behind the newspaper, into his iPad, or in front of a television. I have taken to pointing out to my husband couples in restaurants that sit in stony silence—desperate souls living under the same roof who have lost any commonality that might once have existed. Not them. Not me.

Oddly, the movie didn't seem to interest any of my friends, all of whom refused my invitation to go. Their shared excuse was they had no interest in watching middle-aged sex. That, of course, raised my first red flag. I've come to believe sex (or the lack thereof) is the best-kept secret in most American households. If couples aren't wondering what happened to their desire, they're wondering if it's normal not to have any desire. For sure everyone is wondering who is having sex, who isn't, how often, and what's supposed to be the norm, anyway? But no one's talking, and what's more, hardly anyone is telling the truth.

Thankfully Meryl was. Her character seemed determined to change her circumstances regardless of the outcome. "I'd rather be alone than lonely," she told the therapist who specialized in reigniting burnt-out relationships. "But I don't just want to 'do it.' I want to be noticed, to be loved, to feel special."

Amen, I practically said aloud.

The term "doing it" has never done it for me, either. It reminds me of an experience in Philadelphia. I was walking down the hallway of a hotel when I heard guttural sounds coming from Room 413. Not wanting to seem the voyeur, yet fascinated by the various ohs, aahs, and grunts emitting from behind the door, I stopped in my tracks and imagined the scene on the other side. This went on for about a minute or two longer when, all of a sudden, silence. But only for a moment. Before I could even step away, the television had snapped on and a football game was in progress. What had become of the climactic moment? Where had the afterglow gone? Was this all, or was this "it"?

My sex life began 45 years ago in East Africa, where mosquito netting hung from the ceiling over two twin beds. The choice I had on my wedding night was either to get together and sweat it out or risk being eaten by bugs certain to carry malaria. Romantic it was not, and our conjugal life got off to an awkward start. It didn't help that we were perfect strangers, having known each other for only a few months in college.

Like the therapist in the movie suggested, we tried exercises to initiate sexual intimacy, and we got better at "it" throughout the years, but something was often lacking.

"Women are lonely, and men just don't get it," said a happily divorced friend who actually went to see the movie. Although she didn't love the film, she noted the theme spoke loudly about why she was relieved to have gotten out. "A relationship is not about sex and blow jobs," she espoused. "Relationship is about relating, which happens to be a verb. Couples need to take action beyond the bedroom—as simple as listening to each other, holding hands, or going to bed at the same time."

While recently away at a girls' weekend—where we indulged in nonstop chatter without censoring—the topic of our sex lives came up, as it inevitably does.

"What sex life?" my friend Vera exhaled in her lovely southern drawl. "Hank has a dead dick!"

We gasped, laughing in shock at her frank delivery.

"Well, it's no different at my house," admitted Bonnie, who hadn't had sex for several years. "We never talk about it, but the poor guy is utterly embarrassed. We women get blamed for being cold when the truth is, their equipment's no longer functioning."

"Everyone's equipment is aging out," I piped up. "I suspect women want a break, too. Menopause—a pause from men—get it?"

It's been said that if sex were taken out of the equation more marriages would succeed rather than fail. This does not mean a relationship comes to an end, only that certain aspects shed their skins or lose their shells, disappear without a trace, leave no forwarding address, and then suddenly reappear in a different form. Not that I have an aversion to sex; I just feel it shouldn't play the role of be all and end all.

What I know for sure is love goes through various stages like everything else. The first stage is adolescent love, when the hormones are popping and our partner is new. The second is functional relationship, or staying together because of money, family, and life concerns—all of which dim the flame considerably. Finally there is adult love, when you have the freedom to explore a new life, independent of one another, and bring that excitement back to your mate. This, in turn, reignites the fire. That is, if there's still a desire to do so.

The media mostly focuses on the first stage, ignoring the virtues of long-term commitment. I read an article in *The New York Times* that claimed monogamy is almost impossible, mainly because it was conceived when people lived to be 40, not 80.

Meanwhile, my dear friend Sylvia ended her second marriage because of adolescent love. "I thought I was in love when, in fact, it was only lust. I say only, because lust is temporary," she said. "It never lasts. It's just a physical fulfillment. By choosing lust over love, I lost a decent man and the respect of four children."

A Hollywood producer once suggested that love affairs take as much time as preparing and serving a gourmet meal. The same is true for fine-tuning your golf game or orchestrating any major family event. Yet most of us don't have the inclination to plan a sexual interlude after a day, or years, of mundane living. If the Chinese are right—that regular sex is paramount to good health—then perhaps we should be trained in the art of "doing it." Surely the pharmaceutical companies aren't preparing us properly by insisting that for a man to be ready when the time is right, he need only take a pill.

Though the question remains: what does sex have to do with it? I think lots of affection, coupled with respect and interest in each other's lives, is the basis for a strong relationship. Toss in a significant amount of hugging, which is known to boost the immune system, and you really have something going for you.

As hormones shift and age creeps in, my hope is that couples can love each other enough to go from being simply sexual to delightfully sensual. They are, after all, in many ways interchangeable. And from that, who knows what might spring forth. The pleasure is all yours.

11

Loving
Unconditionally

S T R E T C H I N G

toward ACCEPTANCE

LOVING UNCONDITIONALLY

Not long after my mother passed away I visited a friend's house for lunch, where she proudly dished up steaming bowls of homemade vegetable soup—the perfect complement to a cold winter's day. As a group of us took our places around the table, our hostess lifted her spoon to the woman who raised her and sipped to the delicious recipe she'd left behind.

Without warning I blurted out just how much I missed my mother. "Not her presence so much," I explained, wiping away the tears, "but the unconditional love."

Instead of a tableful of understanding nods I was met with a few blank stares. Some women had never experienced unconditional maternal love. Either their mothers had been punitive and critical, or they were so disappointed in their own lives that they had little joy left to impart to their daughters. Many wished their mothers could have been better role models or, at the very least, have had the guts to be their own persons.

That was my mother: gutsy, as well as someone who never seemed to age out. Up until her death at 94, her favorite motto remained *nothing ventured, nothing gained.* Although she was raised in a tiny, cold-water flat in Brooklyn, where she shared a bedroom with her brother, she created her own space by lining shoeboxes with wallpaper. If she couldn't have her own dresser, she would make one. Always looking for the next opportunity, she lied about her age to get a job on Wall Street, where she learned everything she needed to know about investing in order to grow a decent portfolio from my father's meager paycheck. She was an enterprising striver for sure, always reaching for the next rung on the ladder.

Even more remarkable, with each dainty step her style remained impeccable. Our various houses seeped from the pages of *Better Homes and Gardens*, and her keen attention to detail was evidenced in her color-coordinated wardrobe, to say nothing of her size 12 figure.

When her own kids came along, she was equally as aggressive with devotion. She once drove five hours in a blinding snowstorm when she heard I was in the college infirmary. And in my adult years, when she was well into her 90s, she followed the ambulance to a hospital in the middle of the night after I'd broken my ankle. Talk about unconditional love! No matter what was happening in her life, she would rush to the rescue.

If I were to be completely honest, though, there certainly were moments in which she loved me *with condition:* the frequent comments about my chubby body, warnings about unladylike behavior, being more than pushy about getting good grades, and suggestions about how to behave around men so I could capture one.

As the luncheon conversation shifted from our mothers to our own mothering, it occurred to me that conditional love stems from fear or embarrassment. Looking back, I can see how my mother was trying to steer me in directions that would give me what she hadn't gotten or help me avoid disappointments along the way. Wasn't that what I did with my own children? When one dyed his hair orange and grew a ponytail, I was so embarrassed I wouldn't attend anything by his side. I also not-so-gently encouraged the boys to graduate from college with honors so they could secure even better futures. To their credit, they both seemed delighted when they disappointed me.

Unspoken expectations are a more subtle way of expressing conditional love—nothing is demanded outright, but a fine print exists none-the-less. When our egos step aside, unconditional love reigns. Hopefully, I've been able to do this enough that my boys trust I'll always be there for them when they need me. Unfortunately, at times my conditions have clouded my efforts.

When one of the boys came home for a visit, obviously distraught by circumstances in his family, job, and finances, I watched as his mood tumbled. He never once beckoned to me for an opinion or a solution. That night I tossed and turned until finally flipping on the light and putting a pen to paper. Without judgment or motive, I wrote what was on my heart. In the morning he read my letter, and over a cup of coffee we had a great discussion—a real coming together like in the old days.

"No one can go it alone," I ventured to say. "Now that we've talked, let's keep the dialogue going via email. I'm always writing, and you hardly answer."

"Well, I might not answer in the future, either," he replied.

"Huh?" I was astounded. Hadn't we just crossed a mother-son sharing threshold?

"Don't you understand?" he said. "You're about the only person in the world I can disappoint."

A poignant response but a hard one for a mother to hear.

I once met a woman in Costa Rica who concluded that while her daughter's choices are not what she would have chosen, she's learned to support her daughter in who she is becoming. What would my life feel like if I made no more demands, wishes, expectations, or requirements? What if I gave up judgment and accepted those I love without reason—a tall order, but one that would offer me grace and relief?

The poet Rumi wrote, "The task is not to seek Love, but rather to seek and find all the barriers within ourselves that we have built against Love."

Love keeps no records of wrongs, and it ignores habits, patterns, and mistakes. One day, when my children are sitting around a table discussing my love, I don't want them to remember my conditions. I want them to remember my *unconditions*—and feel as grateful for my love as I do for my mother's.

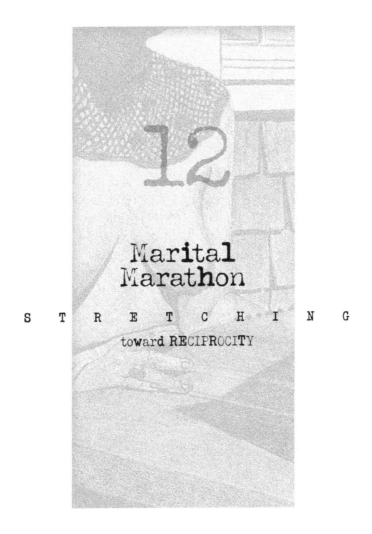

12

Marital Marathon

S T R E T C H I N G

toward RECIPROCITY

MARITAL MARATHON

One hot and humid day in July, my husband and I headed north to crew for our son Andy in the Vermont 100, an endurance foot race of 100 miles. Crazy, I admit, but an extreme sport our son discovered some 15 years ago all the same. Because this race was on the East Coast we were able to become part of his supporting team— something we hadn't been for a while.

To help him hydrate, eat, and otherwise function while scissoring his legs more than halfway across a state (Vermont is 159 miles north to south), we were to be his handlers. Our job literally was to manage his gear, then hand him what he needed along the way.

Packed in the trunk of our car waited a cooler full of ice, organic turkey, avocadoes, Greek yogurt, ginger tablets, bouillon cubes, a drink named Succeed, and a disgusting energy slime he called goop. He'd given us a detailed list, knowing precisely the nourishment his body would need to run such a race.

We arrived in the middle of the night with the theme from *Chariots of Fire* blaring over the PA system. The vacant farmland overflowed with 300 excited runners stretching, gulping coffee, and cheering each other on. In the corner of a large tent sat a few lone souls privately meditating. We spotted Andy glad-handing old competitors as relaxed as if he were at a cocktail party and headed over.

Treading through a swarm of kinetic bodies, the term lean and mean took on a whole new definition. There was no hanging flesh here! Each participant was the sculpted specimen only hours and hours of training could yield. Sucking it in wasn't even worth the effort.

Andy was in good spirits, but as time ticked forward he grew more and more pensive. As 5 a.m. approached, he and all the other able-bodied men and women began migrating toward the starting gate. Their jovial banter had quieted, and the music had been silenced. For a split second only the hum of cicadas remained. Then the gun blared, and the horde was propelled into darkness with nothing but headlamps to light the way. We would not see our athlete again for three hours, at which point he would have run the equivalent of a marathon.

During the pre-race meeting, we'd been reminded that each runner has his or her own style of survival. "They know what they need," the race director advised. "You, the crew, are there at each aid station to take orders and offer support."

In short, I was playing Mom again. Only this time, my husband was, too.

Days before, Andy had printed a spreadsheet that broke his run into eight splits. From this we knew when to expect him and exactly what he would need at each station. He appeared at the first stop on schedule, one of three at the head of the pack. Amazingly focused, his eyes said *get me my nourishment without breaking my stride*. He slowed to a brisk walk, spooning yogurt into his mouth while his father ran alongside him with packets of goop and two freshly filled water bottles. In less than 30 seconds he was down the road and out of sight like the Road Runner of cartoon fame.

With adrenaline flowing, we jumped back into the car and sped off to the next station, discussing how we could streamline our function while trying to navigate the country roads of rural Vermont. Upon arrival, we staked out a space amidst other handlers and spectators, then sat and waited. When we spotted the top of his sweaty head bobbing up and down, we prepared for another sprint.

This went on throughout the day, but as the temperature climbed, the crowd of handlers thinned. By midday many runners had either cramped or dropped. A veteran, Andy continued to arrive at each stop within minutes of when his timesheet predicted, albeit hot and tired.

At mile 75, he was joined by a pacer—a morale booster who understands both the challenge and the course. His job was to encourage Andy to stay in the hunt when he started to wonder why the hell he was doing it in the first place. "It's lonely out there," we'd heard our son say. "Especially if you're ahead of the pack and barely see another soul."

Between runner appearances some collegiality developed among us handlers. When we weren't preparing food and drinks, we shared nervous chatter regarding our athletes' quirks, training programs, race schedules, and the ever-present question of why they do it at all. On this particular day there was a lone husband who stood ready with two portable coolers and medical supplies, as well as a very pregnant wife who dutifully handed her husband a secret concoction at each stop, followed by purple goop.

As we bandaged and fed our delirious and dazed charges, I was reminded that no man is an island, and it occurred to me that ultramarathons are a good metaphor for life. Although we go it alone, those who have the greatest success have a team behind them. The more we prepare, train, accept help, and set realistic goals, the better we will fare.

Looking over at my husband as he loped next to our son with an avocado in hand and concentration furrowing his brow, it also occurred to me that marriage may be the biggest endurance race of all.

Most couples start their life together with the hope of finishing in some mutually desirable manner. Yet that can only happen if they nourish each other's dreams, lead cheers when the other is down, work together to overcome mountains and valleys, and become each other's pacer at the 75-mile mark.

Long-time marriages begin to crumble when support wanes or few accolades or trophies are left to look forward to—especially as the end of the race nears. Only the best of pacers can help with life's hurdles.

Andy crossed the finish line as a winner, and I realized that if a couple put that kind of effort and determination into a marriage, they might not only finish the race together, they may actually win it.

That night, after I shared my new insights with my husband, he rolled over and smiled through his exhaustion.

"As long as I don't have to eat any of that goop," he said, "I'm in."

13

Ripping the Velcro

S T R E T C H I N G

toward LETTING GO

RIPPING THE VELCRO

The long-awaited day had arrived. We loaded our son's belongings into the car, stripped his bedroom walls of memorabilia, and drove off to college as though it was just another family vacation. Up until that moment I hadn't thought much about how his leaving would affect our family, but as the distance between his old home and his new one grew, the reality seeped in—one less person at the dinner table, a half-empty calendar once cluttered with sporting events, and our younger son more like an only child.

Never mind, I chastised myself. We were participating in a rite of passage, an inevitable step on his road to adulthood, and I was intent on putting a positive spin on the activities of the next 24 hours. I would stay eagerly engaged in the experience: his first big launch.

There was much to do once we arrived on campus— unpacking a station wagon, settling into his antiquated dorm room, meeting helpful upper classmen, looking over his schedule, buying supplies—all distracting chores that kept me in the moment. It wasn't until we headed for the convocation that I fully realized what was happening. As new students were directed to one side of the gym and families to the other, something inside me tore. We were participating in the act of *moving in* when, in reality, the *moving on* was in process.

It's OK, I told myself. Wasn't I anxious to get out from under my parents' tutelage at that age? To be free from their rules, to get on with my independent life, to become someone new? I put on a brave face, not wanting to be seen as one of those clinging, doting couples known as "Velcro parents."

Once the program ended, the matriculating students stayed put while the families were ushered into the chapel. After a few opening remarks, the dean gently attempted to tell us everything was about to change. Our children no longer were children, but rather men and women in their own right.

"Their social life, as well as their academic life, will be between your children and us," she explained. "Any issues they have while here at the college are confidential unless your son or daughter gives us permission to inform you."

Talk about ripping apart the Velcro, if not a final cutting of the umbilical cord. And for God's sake, we were still paying the bills! A quick glance at a few other mothers told me I wasn't the only one pitting parental prerogative against separation anxiety.

I tried to stay present, but as the minutes slipped away so did our family as I knew it. With her sobering lecture filling my already heavy heart, saying farewell to my eldest felt akin to wrapping an anchor around my waist and flinging my body into the campus retention pond.

He met us at the car to grab his golf bag and give me an awkward hug, careful not to make eye contact. As much as I wanted him to need me, his body language read *onward*. There were new friends to make, a singing group and a golf team to try out for, and, of course, a new crop of girls.

Watching him stroll across campus toward the "Men's Residence," it was clear he was walking out of one life and into another. We had launched him, and now life experience would take over. He would be forced into an allegiance with a new community—and with no more influence by us. In a flash, it was sayonara to childhood, and motherhood.

I hadn't counted on the day being so raw, nor did I expect to be so completely altered. With a brief adieu, I'd evolved into someone who had little to do with the boy she had reared and raised.

"Have a nice time in college," I shrieked between sobs, hanging out of the car window in one final obligatory moment of embarrassment.

By the time we got home I was emotionally exhausted. Not only was the farewell harrowing, but during the drive I'd worked diligently on a list of ploys to keep him attached. I would write once a week, send creative care packages, and count the days until Parents Weekend. Yes, I knew my actions were pathological, but after 20 years of being Mom, I was entitled to a little mourning.

Perhaps somewhere inside I recognized there would be many stages of grief ahead, as well as another day, just like that one, in which I'd say goodbye to our younger son. One final rip.

Looking back now, it's hard to believe a good two-thirds of my life has been inextricably intertwined with my two sons. Without question I was a mother hen, taking pride in my progeny while pushing them to bright futures. As such, retiring from motherhood the second time had not been my finest moment.

Suddenly there were *two* vacant bedrooms, a family dinner table set for two instead of four, and as time went on, fewer phone calls and less contact. Having an empty nest had never been on my wish list, and a momentary, if not perpetual, hole in my heart formed.

On good days I refer to the role of motherhood as something simply outlived. We have our kids for about 20 years, and then it's over. A natural progression of the life cycle. On bad days, the child within me pretends nothing ever ends, and because of her, it has taken me far too long to accept the inevitable.

Kahlil Gibran advises parents in his book *The Prophet*:

[Children] come through you but not from you,

And though they are with you yet they belong not to you.

You may give them your love but not your thoughts,

For they have their own thoughts.

You may house their bodies but not their souls,

For their souls dwell in the house of tomorrow,

which you cannot visit, not even in your dreams.

Although I know all of this intellectually, the letting go process doesn't just happen one fall day when a person's effects are transported from one life to another. It's a releasing in degrees, much like Velcro is hundreds of little loops breaking free from hundreds of little hooks.

A good friend suggested that raising a child results in the one relationship that, if you do a good job, ends in separation. Well into adulthood my sons have outlived the arms of their mother, and it seems I am to simply bless them when they come and release them when they go.

It occurs to me that I have been dwelling too much on what's changed and not enough on what's lasting. Perhaps it is time to delight not in what they are doing, but who they are—enthusiasts for sure, and full of bombastic energy. These tough warriors and independent men are moving forward, not backward, with humor and resilience. Now I need to do the same.

Again from *The Prophet*:

We are the bows from which our children, as living arrows, are sent forth.

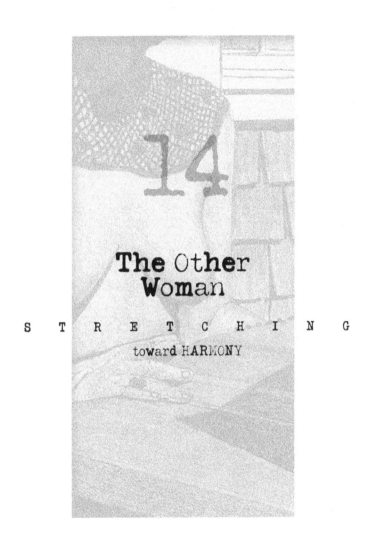

14

The Other Woman

STRETCHING

toward HARMONY

THE OTHER WOMAN

Sixteen years ago, when our son walked down the aisle and said, "I do," so did I. Having never had a daughter, I was ready for another woman in the family, and I was determined to make the relationship work.

While I never expected to become best friends, having a girlfriend with whom I could sit and chat over a glass of wine seemed reasonable. I was quick to discover, however, that daughters-in-law are a peculiar breed of female who, if they happen to have a living mother, don't want another such person in their lives. There's also a modicum of mistrust around the mother-in-law, as she is all but expected to meddle. But I would be a model mother-in-law, I promised myself, and create a totally different dynamic.

From the beginning, my modus operandi was never to be like those awful mother-in-law jokes frequently told by stand-up comedians. The most insulting I've ever heard was about two men reading the back of a wine bottle. *It's full-bodied, imposing, with a nutty base, a sharp bite, and a bitter aftertaste,* one said. *Sounds like my mother-in-law,* the other replied.

No way. I never wanted that kind of characterization applied to me. To ensure it wasn't, my secret pledge was to never, *ever* be nosey, invasive, or pushy—three attributes I've been known to exude. Instead, I would be gracious, fun loving, and helpful, just to name a few.

This would not be easy, I knew. Far from meek, such a resolve meant muzzling my feelings and stifling controversial conversations, but I was prepared to do what was needed to create good energy. What I wasn't prepared for was the confounding complexity of my task.

My newly married son and daughter-in-law were visiting one weekend when they chose to stay out all night. The next day I learned they'd been partying with a bunch of our son's old cronies. Thinking only of her feelings, I chastised him openly. "And you dragged your young wife along?!" Minutes later, she confronted me. Standing in the driveway with her hands on her hips, she made it clear that I had no business taking HER HUSBAND to task. Ever.

The fear of God was shocked into me that very day, and I immediately was rendered odd woman out—not to mention speechless. Knowing my tendencies, I tried other avenues of expression over the years, such as sending thoughtful gifts, flowers, and notes. Yet few of these ploys worked miracles, even after my second daughter-in-law joined the ranks. Being "maid to order" was the only way to gain points. I flew cross-country numerous times for the birth of each child, happy to do laundry and make meals. For once I felt needed, and it was wonderful to be a part of these newly forming families. It seemed unnatural to not belong, always sitting on the sidelines waiting to be called upon. But once my presence became a burden, it was back to the bench.

I'd grown so distressed over the ever-widening gap between these women and me that I called together a group of friends to see if we could gain clarity on this sticky subject. As it turned out, they too were suffering in silence about the "in-law issue." We all admitted (particularly if we had sons) that we'd received pink slips for mothering on the day of the wedding, not the hall passes we'd originally anticipated.

In fear of losing complete connection with our offspring, we also confessed to some fancy in-law footwork, twisting ourselves up like pretzels to not judge, insult, intrude, or be misconstrued. The general agreement was if we made one wrong move, then the door leading to passed-down recipes, spoiled grandchildren, and family gatherings might forever be slammed in our faces.

In retrospect, it all might have been a grand case of paranoia. Or, better yet, unrealistic expectations. The Chinese character for conflict is a picture of two women under the same roof. Then there's the Bible, which states that a man leaves his mother and cleaves to his wife. Combine these two tidbits with the historical observation that a man's not capable of loving more than one woman at a time, and perhaps we mothers are meant to bow out gracefully.

Alright...but completely?!

Instead of feeling depressed and resigned, I spent a weekend in the Harvard Library researching the in-law relationship and how to make it work. Interestingly, most international cultures have a defined place in the family structure for elders and in-laws. Most, that is, except America.

So imagine my delight when an article appeared in the Sunday paper about how President Obama's mother-in-law had moved into the White House. Called "the family mainstay," this woman was raising eyebrows. The male reporter relayed how several presidents have been *forced* to ponder the delicate and sometimes unpleasant question of whether or not to move the in-laws into the White House. The tone of the article suggested the mother-in-law's presence might endanger, rather than enhance, the first couple's marriage. A familial interloper she could possibly become! Still, it was a relief to hear how this tough-minded matriarch was valued—despite the fact that she didn't keep her mouth shut. (May that be a subtle permission for the rest of us!)

So obsessed was I by this topic that I talked with my publisher about writing a book on the subject. Unfortunately, most of the editors I reached out to disliked their mothers-in-law enough to have zero interest in working on such a manuscript. Mostly in their 30s and 40s, these women saw no possibility for an amicable relationship with their mothers-in-law, so why would they want to waste their time thinking about it?

Somewhat defeated, I've concluded the in-law conundrum is basically unfixable, doomed from the get-go bound as the two women are, not by desire, but by law.

The only positive note is that it's no one's fault. Yet, if I could have a do-over, I would suggest a yearly luncheon with my daughters-in-law to talk about how I was faring. Instead of a pink slip or a hall pass, this would be a report card. And there, in black and white, I would know where I excelled and where I fell short. At least then I wouldn't have to skulk around in wonder, a student of my own reluctance.

You know what? Maybe I should ask. Now if only I knew how to word the invitation...

15

The Children
Are Getting a
Divorce

S   T   R   E   T   C   H   I   N   G

toward FORGIVENESS

THE CHILDREN ARE GETTING
A DIVORCE

No one has died, thank God, but there is a divorce happening in the family—a completely unexpected occurrence that has left my heart pounding. A different kind of death. Our son phoned one cold February morning, his voice strange and fragile. I motioned to my husband, who was nestled in his easy chair reading the morning *Times,* to pick up the extension. Right. Now.

What we heard was not pretty.

"I want a divorce," our son whispered. "My marriage is over."

I leaned against the wall, struggling to harness my shallow breathing. With each exhale I filled the dead air with questions: "What about therapy? Are you sure this is what it's come to? You seemed reasonably happy last summer…" I so badly wanted to tell him, flat out, that divorce was not an option if for no other reason than he couldn't afford it. But I zipped my lip and grabbed a pen to take notes. I didn't want my shock to erase the truth coming across the wire. In lockstep, my husband pulled out a legal pad and began scribbling a list of the consequences of divorce.

Without realizing it, we'd shifted immediately into the five stages of grief developed by American psychiatrist Elisabeth Kübler-Ross. This couldn't be happening in our family, I thought. Stage one—denial. "Why didn't you reach out to us?" I screamed. "Or get some help?" Stage two—anger. By the end of the 55-minute phone call, we were simply bargaining—stage three—as we attempted to slow things down, change the course of action, and make a difference some way, somehow. When we hung up the phone, the fourth stage—depression—had begun to creep in.

That's what happens when real-life storms appear. No time to prepare, just zippo; you're thrust into hardship, pain, and grief.

I obsessed about nothing other than divorce for the next six months, interviewing divorcees and mothers in my position, talking to lawyers, going to therapy, and reading book after book on the subject. It was the latter that depressed me the most. They all affirmed that divorce is a crazy time. What's more, the chaos lasts an average of five years. Five years more of this! Of nothing making sense to anyone. Of the tension and the tears. The visitations and the hurried exchanges. Even worse, no matter which perspective you hold—partner, parent, grandparent, child, sibling—there's no escaping it. The decision affects everyone and all relationships, and there's no preparation for how to deal with each individual's complex, confused feelings.

This fixer mom was finally rendered powerless. There was no waving a magic wand over this situation, no rewriting the scenario I ached to see. Indeed, I couldn't even pray him out of this dilemma. Still, I felt the need to smooth the waters and swab away his pain.

It's too easy to get married, I kept saying, and oh, so hard to get divorced. Could I have done something to stop it? Thinking back to their wedding preparations, I remember questioning why they skipped out of pre-marital counseling in favor of a one-day, Pre-Cana lecture, where multitudes of engaged couples learned of the experience upon which they were about to embark. Having no power in their decision I couldn't insist on more deliberation, so I took it as a good omen when five priests surrounded them during the ceremony.

"If this marriage doesn't survive," I joked to a friend, "no marriage would."

As the news of our mess got around, my e-mail flooded with advice and horror stories. I gained slight comfort in knowing we weren't alone. Other than the hurt and pain of watching a family break apart, they shared stories of personal abrasions that matched mine—being chastised for asking benign questions, giving lectures, transferring my pain onto them, laying guilt trips, and enduring the deafening silence when they would go remote.

"No dialogue makes my imagination go wild," said one woman. "Then FEAR kicks in…False Evidence Appearing Real." The hurts just keep coming, and the child supposes the mother can endure. One finally said she gave it to God, while another threw the requests for psychic and economic help into the too-hard-even-for-God pile.

No doubt parental love is potentially the purest form of love, but it might also be the most painful. "We must give those we love their independence," said Sister Wendy Beckett. "We cannot make their choices for them; they cannot live by our hard-earned experience. This is part of love." It's true. It's his life, and no one can change the path he's on—not even his mother!

Yet there's something to be said for the wisdom I've gained by living in a well-tested marriage. Surely I had something to add. They didn't even see how far the effects of their divorce reached, loaded down as they were by their own pain, shame, broken dreams, and loss of direction.

My therapist was able to get through to my desperation when she explained, "Women often believe the more they obsess over a situation, the more they can actually change the outcome." I burst out laughing and crying at the same time, both because it made such sense and because I'd spent a lifetime obsessing.

I remember being told by my sister-in-law during her and my brother's divorce that she would have nothing more to say to me, as she was divorcing the entire family. Having been her roommate in college and a good friend for 20 years, I felt like she had died, and I couldn't even attend a funeral to say goodbye. It was simply over from her viewpoint. At least the Japanese have what they call a divorce ritual. The two families come together and listen as each half of the couple explains what was worthy in their union and what didn't work. They then burn their marriage license, and it's over.

No doubt, divorce sucks. It's an ongoing roller coaster ride. One day it seems it will all work out, and the next day the world feels damaged beyond repair. But just when I felt I couldn't take anymore, providence appeared.

I was reading my morning devotional when I came across a line that hit me between the eyes: *Be free in your spirit always...do not waste time attaching yourself to hurt and pain.* Having been raised in a fear-based household, I frequently attach to the negative rather than the positive, even though I know better. As I pondered the quote, I focused on the word attach—something that denotes clinging rather than letting go. I was holding onto that which was not serving, but in truth destroying, me. Instead, time could be better spent enjoying the moment or engaging in the process of what we were doing. Letting go of hoped-for destinations or outcomes that were almost unattainable seemed like a good step toward healing.

The very same day my cousin called for no other reason than to remind me that our son had reached out to her at the very beginning of this situation to ask that she take care of me in my distress.

Put down the weight and walk to the other side, Joan, I said to myself. *Time's up. Write yourself back into your life! Be hospitable to the stranger that is you.*

It's been four years of denial, anger, bargaining, and grief, and we are finally at the stage of acceptance...well, almost. While I've come to the conclusion that I didn't cause the divorce—and I certainly can't fix it—I rationalize the entire ordeal with Carl Jung's belief that half of life is not to be understood. The familiar foundation of marriage was taken away only to be replaced by something new.

"We shape ourselves to fit the world, and by the world we are shaped again," wrote David Whyte in his poem *Working Together*.

Wake up now. The long night is past and gone.

16

The Truth Is Rarely Spoken Because the Time Is Never Right

S T R E T C H I N G

toward FINDING TIME

THE TRUTH IS RARELY SPOKEN
BECAUSE THE TIME IS NEVER RIGHT

Over the river and through the woods, we were headed for a family Thanksgiving. For several days we'd be huddled in our son's farmhouse in rural Virginia cooking, peeling apples, baking pies, and chopping wood. Meanwhile, football games would abound on television and outside on the vast fields. Such a time is a silent invitation into vulnerability. When you visit your grown children you must be open and available to the rhythm of their lives. Frankly, there is no other way.

Even so, there are always expectations. I can't help it. What I think I am going toward is not necessarily what I'm going to meet. This time I actually voiced a few desires— wine tasting at Donald Trump's winery, dinner at a favorite Chinese restaurant, and attending a grandson's basketball game so we could cheer him on, view the school culture, and meet a few of the boys' friends. Then there were the unspoken desires—intense conversations, sharing, and growth. These rare and precious get-togethers are yet another chance to know each other, and we go into the moment and stay at the center having learned there is no intimacy found at the periphery.

Seeing each son so infrequently, time has to be taken to settle into each other's energy, but mostly, it's delightful just to be a family. When we're not all engaged together, I sit on the stairwell landing pretending to read a book when, in fact, I'm observing, listening, and eavesdropping on cell phone calls or chuckling at brotherly jokes. As time goes on, I'm dying to know more. Once a reporter, I was trained to probe into the lives and situations of others. It's not that I'm nosey, I just believe the oral tradition is the most valuable way to learn.

Of course, therein lies the trouble. My children are certain something they say will end up in one of my books. And, indeed, it often does, but only because the lessons they teach me are the gems other parents want to know. The truth is, I'm addicted to curiosity and adore reciprocating. Being asked questions to which I can offer my opinions provides me extreme pleasure, especially when those queries come from my sons. Being able to ask questions—and receive an answer in return—is sheer rapture.

It used to be so easy when we all lived under the same roof. My questions could be answered by simply looking in their directions or observing the way they walked into the house. But now they live so far away I don't have the luxury of casual connection, in which mundane talks can give a mother a clue as to what's going on in their lives. Tidbits they post on Facebook don't offer much backstory, and texts tell me they're alive, but that's about all.

Sometimes I question my expectations and feel as though I'm holding on to something that simply isn't mine anymore. Am I being unreasonable? Perhaps not. Jungian therapist Florida Scott-Maxwell writes of her feelings, "No matter how old a mother is, she watches her middle-aged children for signs of improvement, never outgrowing the burden of love and the weight of hope for those she bore."

Certainly my boys were and are the most important characters in my story. As such, I am not ready to give up and know them only as loved strangers. How to get to know the real them is the question.

I've pretty well mastered honest argumentation with friends, but family is another issue altogether. While we're all fortunately on the same page politically, the nuances of frank conversation trip me up. It has taken a lot of inner undoing and me pulling back from the way I was as their mother, saying what was on my mind without censoring.

The cruel fact is there are no more teachable moments. They no longer are beholden to their parents' ideals or standards. Instead, they've married or merged their values with another's. They thrive in a free state far from their original home with an emboldened knowledge that is theirs, not ours. Anything that reeks of control will send them packing.

One son understands soul talk while the other runs from it. But if they don't have anything positive to report in their lives, they don't talk at all about what might be going wrong. Apparently they've subtly shifted into full-fledged manhood whether they're actually there yet or not.

So how to bridge this gap, widening like a barrier beach once the ocean has broken through, growing larger with each new storm?

Whoever said *the truth is rarely spoken because the time is never right* hit the nail on the head. I've concluded that shared communication can only occur when the time and place are right. And even then, improvisation is required to get the ball rolling.

Recently I heard a well-known poet speak on the art of courageous conversations. He explained how he waited for the perfect time to insert himself in a reciprocal talk with his only son. "I was driving him off to college some six hours away, and I figured it was my last chance to know him as a kid before we said sayonara to his youth. So not an hour into the ride I asked him, 'What it was like to have your childhood with us?'" That was a showstopper! Either his son wanted to climb out of the car at the nearest gas station, or he really got into his story. I would have given anything to be in the backseat listening.

Most mothers report that sons are the hardest with which to converse. "Usually I hear from him as he's driving home from work. It feels as if he is sneaking around to talk to me," one explained. "Suddenly the garage door goes up, and click, the phone is off."

The difficult hurdle is to not ask questions that could be heard as judgments: Do you really like your job? Why would you invest in real estate in a poor school district? You're going where? Is she really the one? The minute they smell judgment the conversation heats up or goes dead. Delivery is also important. Concentrating hard to sound and be interested usually makes for a decent call. Shifting my tone from desperate curiosity to laid-back inquiry works, as well.

I also started paying close attention to where conversations took place and found it easier to really talk while staring off across the ocean at the beach or driving in a car.

So there I had it: topic, tone, and timing—or waiting for those moments when I could casually jump in. Creating the proper combination was the key to honest conversation.

It's all so tedious. Once powerful in the family as mothers and fathers we begin to tiptoe, and our children don't realize we feel marginalized and dismissed. I've concluded the time will never be right. The only solution is one I heard mentioned by Meryl Streep during a television interview over the holidays. The host asked her what she'd like for Christmas.

She wrinkled up her nose and pondered the question for a split second. "I would like to spend one whole day with each of my children anytime this coming year and just be together to catch up."

I could have jumped through the television to give her a high five for the affirmation that caring for connection and conversation with my offspring is totally normal. I have no intention of crawling into the casket without knowing who my kids are becoming. Yes, tact and truth take time, but somehow in the New Year I hope to find just that. For as the Bible proclaims: *Ask and it shall be given.*

Facing the future

We already possess everything
we need to move forward.
Each of us has inherited all
the bold vision, the courage,
the compassion,
and the integrity required
to repair our lives and spirits.

17

The Game Changer

S T R E T C H I N G

toward BREAKING THE RULES

THE GAME CHANGER

A half hour into a game of Scrabble it became apparent the letters before me would not spell a thing. The hearth was offering soft warmth to combat the outside chill, but my internal temperature alone could have heated the room. Still, being a stubborn sort, I refused to give up.

Certainly there was a two-letter word I could play! I tried piecing my tiles together in various combinations, making up words in the process: TZ, DG, HX, TQ, ZX. As the minutes ticked away, and my husband sighed one time too many, a drop of sweat slid from underneath my breast. When the second fell, I did what the world proclaims one should never, ever, *ever* do: I gave up. Dumping my seven consonants back into the pile, I forfeited my turn and picked a fresh bunch.

After a flash of defeat mingled with relief, my temperature returned to normal and my husband's breathing leveled. Even better, I was gifted with numerous possibilities. As the wind howled, the game took off with newfound energy and rejuvenated spirits.

It occurred to me as we continued to play that I could do myself a favor by applying this rule to life. More frequently should I toss out those events and situations that, after much probing and pondering, simply don't work anymore. Instead of holding on to outcomes, attitudes, and people, the more prudent solution would be to create a fresh slate.

I'd recently done just that by dropping out of a woman's sharing group. The point of our monthly meetings was to discuss issues middle-aged women faced—especially subjects no one had ever dared talk about before. But not only did it take one long, arduous year to gain trust among the women, we never did delve into any of those meaty discussions—the sole reason I was there! I'm ashamed to admit that it took me more than two years to quit.

After our Scrabble game—in which we managed a combined score of 576 points!—I looked at the rulebook. Turns out you don't need to dump all of your letters; you can choose to simply replace only those that aren't working for you. Had I known this, I would have kept the Q...though it did validate a different decision I'd recently made.

Bereft over a diminished friendship, I'd asked a mutual friend if she too had experienced such treatment. "Oh my, yes," she said with a knowing smile, "You're no longer the flavor of the month." Momentarily feeling the fool, I was relieved at once to both know the truth and be freed from further illusion.

Shortly thereafter, a Hertz shuttle driver who proved to be quite the philosopher shared this affirming wisdom: "When someone treats you like an option, and you've always treated them as a priority, it's time to let them go."

Then my estranged friend called me apologetically the next month and asked to take me for lunch. I was torn. We *did* have fun together. Did our friendship really have to be all or nothing? Couldn't we still occasionally get together and enjoy each other's company?

I accepted.

Some situations merit the dumping of two or three letters while others require you to pitch out the whole bunch. The key is to know what to eliminate in order to keep yourself in the game—just make sure it's a game you want to play.

The temptation is to hold on to whatever you have because it's known. The hard part is rattling the cage, taking the leap, and embracing change.

The future is always blowing in.

.

18

Sign Language

S T R E T C H I N G

toward DREAMS

SIGN LANGUAGE

Huffing and puffing through the dunes on my morning beach walk, I came across a sign at a local seaside resort:

Go confidently in the direction of your dreams. Live the life you've imagined.

I chuckled when I realized it was Henry David Thoreau. Seeing as how he believed in simple living it seemed ironic the most posh club in town would quote him. Still, reading this sentiment led me to ponder what it really means to dream, a subject to which I'd not given much thought. I was stunned to realize I couldn't recall the last time I'd actually had a dream—or dared to dream for that matter.

My pace quickened as I anxiously hoofed it home, eager to research the very word dream. Why as we grow older, or "grow up," does our very confidence in dreams seem to diminish? Is dreaming a state of mind reserved only for the youth? Surely when I was younger they came easier and more often.

Once inside, I poured through the dictionary. To dream, or be a dreamer, means to be an idealist, a romantic, a visionary. As a noun, a dream is a series of thoughts, visions, or feelings that happen during sleep. Or it's an idea or vision created in your imagination that's not real. Or, it's something you've very much wanted to do, or be, or have for a long, long time.

The more I thought about it, the more I realized I did dream, and dream often. But since I lacked confidence my dreams would come true, I'd often let them slide past unnoticed. They were involuntary inspirations that would arrive in split-second images or ideas then disappeared just as quickly. Or they came as random thoughts to enlighten a mood or tease me to a higher level of consciousness before flitting back to the enigma from whence they came.

Why had I begun to let them go?

Years prior, after 30 rejections of my first book, I refused to give up hope. During my daily Spinning class the instructor asked us to picture a dream, and I imagined standing with Oprah Winfrey—me in beige chiffon and her in cream—at the bow of a small boat. We crossed the harbor to a vast beach then feasted on lobster and drank white wine, all the while talking about what it meant to be an unfinished woman. I had this vision day after day, never relinquishing the idea. Not more than six months later, I received my first query from Harpo. Although Oprah and I never did share the ocean, we did get to exchange ideas and offer them to a greater audience on her show.

The best part of dreams is they're ours for the taking.

You need only be open to the fact that you are entitled to your dreams to begin to experience hope. The trick is to keep that confidence up no matter how many defeats.

Whenever I need a lift, I put on John Lennon's album and listen to him sing *Imagine*. His refrain, asking everyone to join him as a dreamer, beckons to all of us.

Dreams are not goals, and they don't have to be grand. What's more, most are attainable if you don't set the bar too high. Sometimes dreams can even surprise us, as one did Bubba Watson when he won the coveted Masters Golf Tournament. When asked if his dream had finally come true, he confessed, "Actually, no. I've never had a dream go this far, so I can't really say it's a dream come true."

That takes me back to my old friend Thoreau. I noticed in my tattered copy of *Walden* the entirety of the quote that got me thinking in the first place: "Go confidently in the direction of your dreams. Live the life you've imagined. You will meet with a success unexpected in the common hours of your day."

By dreaming, expanding our horizons, and being open to what could be, the unexpected is bound to eventually happen. Thoreau insists that we simply have to be alive and awake, unhurried and present. And although I have big dreams involving travel and adventure, it will be within my daily endeavors that a majority of my dreams will come true. From those dreams, fresh dreams will follow, keeping my life full of mystery, wonder, and hope. For as Thoreau also espoused, "When I come to die, I do not want to discover that I have not lived."

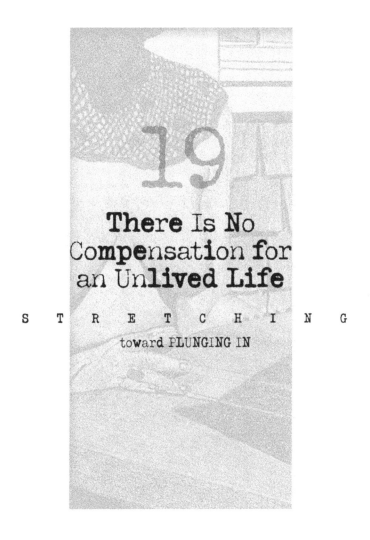

19

There Is No Compensation for an Unlived Life

S T R E T C H I N G

toward PLUNGING IN

THERE IS NO COMPENSATION
FOR AN UNLIVED LIFE

"I'm going to take the plunge," my husband announced as he rolled out of bed on a frigid New Year's Day. He exuded an energy I hadn't seen in decades.

"The what?" I asked, half asleep yet mildly curious.

"Read about it in the paper," he said. "It's a charity event. You pay twenty bucks, go down to our beach, and at noon everyone dives into Nantucket Sound."

"Are you crazy?" I rolled out of bed and headed for the kitchen to put on a pot of coffee. Who was this man? During the cold winter months, he'd spend hours sitting by the hearth wrapped in a blanket dreaming of Florida. Even the slightest drop of temperature turned his extremities frigid. I returned to the bedroom, coffee in hand, expecting to find him curled back up in bed. Instead, he was rummaging through his dresser drawer in search of a bathing suit. He rose victorious then stuffed two beach towels into a plastic bag, mumbling something about this being a New Year's tradition.

"People all over the world take the plunge," he said. "Hell, didn't I tell you the other day that adults learn best when presented with disorienting dilemmas. This should fit the bill."

"Suit yourself," I said as he continued to undress. The word plunge made me think of a plunger—that clever device used to unclog toilets. *Perhaps he feels the need to get unclogged*, I thought.

I threw together bacon and eggs in lieu of the New Year's tradition we did have: brunch with caviar, eggs benedict, smoked salmon, and Bloody Marys. It felt weird, but this man—who had become too laid-back, even lazy— was on a mission. We ate quickly, then wrapped ourselves in Down Jackets, and stepped out into the biting New England air.

At the beach, my wonderment turned to anxiety by the sight of an ambulance standing ready—no doubt to revive anyone struck by shock, heart attack, hypothermia, or any combination of the above. Lined up along the shoreline were 50 or 60 scantily clad men and women waiting to be ridiculous. My husband handed me his coat and joined them.

Something is wrong with this picture, I thought as I crawled into the pocket of a dune to stay warm.

As the clock struck noon in they went, splashing through the shallow water and diving into the deep like a family of polar bears. I stood and scanned the frothing sea to find those familiar limbs, which within five minutes bolted from the water and onto the shore. Shaking my head, I covered his shivering body with towels, and then, the ever-faithful wife, slipped him a shot of single malt Scotch.

Spur-of-the-moment and dumb, this event surely got his adrenaline going. I looked into his wild eyes and reddened cheeks, searching for the husband I knew. What had gotten into him? And how could I get some?

That evening he went on and on about his cold water experience, and I found myself feeling the simpleton.

Was I waiting for something?

It seems I'm always interfering with my own progress by waiting for something, or more accurately, someone—someone to push me along or give me permission or be my companion. Women in my generation were trained in the art of waiting, and I had perfected it: waiting for the suitor to call; waiting to get engaged; waiting to get married; waiting for the baby to arrive; waiting for everyone else's life to be launched so I could launch my own.

It's been years since I've taken any kind of "plunge." Hiking the Inca Trail to Machu Picchu was the last time I took a big risk, and that was eight years ago! I didn't even know where Peru was at the time, but I was intrigued, not to mention filled with an unconscious knowing that it was high time I jumped into the fire.

I actually only did it on a dare to myself. I was sick of hearing about the adventures my kids were having on their bike trips around the world while I sat at home living too normal a life. Besides, I was meant to live through *my* dreams not the dreams of others.

When my cousin invited me to join her and her husband on this amazing Peruvian adventure I was conflicted. "I'll never let you forget what you missed if you don't go," she teased. Still I hesitated. After all, she was a runner and fit, he a vegetarian. And me? I was overweight and under trained—with no hiking experience and no forays into altitude whatsoever. I bought myself a few hours with a lame but plausible excuse, then happened upon a neighbor seven years my senior. Off-hand she told me she couldn't do now what she could do at my age. I bought a ticket to Peru that very day.

Once on the trail I'd hardly expected to be leaping over dead snakes, crawling through slimy tunnels, or creeping across a ravine while balancing on two wobbly logs. But I did it. And I loved it.

Turns out it was one of the chief accomplishments of my life—hiking in altitudes of 14,000 feet, carrying packs, setting up camp, filtering water, and tackling the unknown at every level. On top of it all, no one expected I would actually go through with it, much less revel in the adventure.

A reporter once wrote a story about me entitled *Mess Up Your Life*. Her premise was that the only intelligent thing to do when you hit the wall or reach a major transition is to take a deep breath, face the reality, and leap toward whatever is calling you.

As I've aged out, I've become more careful and less spontaneous. I'm so used to thinking of others first that I frequently pass up dares and chances, and I almost always need a push.

The sand in my sand timer keeps moving through the glass and it never stops, even if I try to ignore it. Recently, I calculated how much time I potentially have left. If I live to be 90, I have 228 more months of life. That's 20 Christmases and probably only 10 more family summer visits. While a tad morbid, the exercise was a good reminder to not waste one more second.

"For the awakened individual, life begins now," said writer Henry Miller. I am beginning to feel a little like Emily in *Our Town* when she returns home from the grave to relive just one day. She is torn both by the beauty of the ordinary and our lack of awareness of it. "Do human beings ever realize life while they live it?" she asks.

This New Year's juncture leaves much unfinished—leftovers from several years past. Having just read about a nurse who worked with people facing life's end, I am thinking of making their sentiments mine:

"I wish I'd had the courage to live a life true to myself, not what others expected of me."

"I wish I hadn't worked so hard."

"I wish I'd had the courage to express my feelings and not settle for peace at all costs."

"I wish I'd let myself be happier, as happiness is a choice."

There remains a mysterious ripening as I move to a new level. My husband's plunge has given me a much needed spontaneity. The reality is that later comes sooner than one thinks. It's way over due, this seizing of my unlived life. I just have to stretch a little further to grasp it.

Stretch a
Little Further
to Grasp It

S T R E T C H I N G

AFTERWARD

Joan Erikson once said life experiences well digested offer the most wisdom. While these essays barely skim the surface of all that has left a mark, message, or value on my existence, I hope they play some small part in affecting yours.

It's the accidental meetings, unexpected events, and surprising suggestions that illuminate epiphanies and bring clarity to the unfinished woman. There are other, less obvious lessons to be found, as well. They won't come on schedule or carry many words. Rather, they will sneak up and surprise you in the form of deeds or gestures I call found blessings.

One such example is of an elderly couple who attends our church. He is tall and stately, while she's hunched over and dazed, a victim of severe dementia. With his arm around her waist or shoulders, he helps her stand or sit, shares the hymnal (although she does not sing or speak), and tends to her every need. His gestures speak of patience, endurance, love, and dedication—taking the wedding vow *in sickness and in health* to a new level. At first I wondered why they were there at all. Sometimes she drools. Other times her body slumps over as if she wants to sleep. But my suspicion is her dedicated husband knows the stimulation of the familiar and the energy of the congregation is precisely what she needs. Such love is out there, but only the continuous seeker stops to pay witness and is moved.

When awake and present, I'm almost always gifted with information that makes me stretch, reach, and go beyond the norm. When I push myself in that way, I move up another rung of the ladder of KNOWING. Again, it's a matter of intention. "Each of us must take charge of our lives unto ourselves," said the poet John Keats.

At my husband's retirement party he told his fellow workers that he was going off to live his "unlived life," a comment that left them dumbfounded. I get the same reaction when I reference being unfinished. One man actually interrupted me mid-sentence to clarify, "You mean, you're unsatisfied, right?"

Wrong.

Most people are working toward an end result—being finished. Being unlived or unfinished, on the other hand, requires work of a different kind. It's based on choices we make when there is still so much to do, to know, and to be. This reality was best illustrated on a business trip to Denver when the hotel housekeeper came to turn down my bed. As I began apologizing for the remnants of a party some friends had thrown in my room, she stopped me. "Play is an important part of the day," she said with a smile. "Don't you know that there are 24 hours—eight for work, eight for sleep, and eight for play? We need all three." This from a hardworking maid who managed three jobs!

For me, it's about joining the community of inquiry— for the goal as I see it is to transcend myself again and again. With the turn of every day I am presented with a vessel full of unused energy. I am driven *to take the current when it serves* as old William Shakespeare said, and then be generative about it.

It amounts to *each one, teach one*, a phrase coined by Dr. Albert Schweitzer, a medical doctor and philosophy guru who practiced in West Africa with the hope that others would follow in his altruistic footsteps. We are all teachers *and* students in this game of life, endowed as we go along with kairos, the Greek term for propitious moments.

Each day of our lives begins with the unknown. That's what gives life its character and texture. The key is to embrace it with perseverance and tenacity. There never will be another day or moment like the one you are living right now. So keep your hearts open and your arms outreached. Everything that comes is a gift.

DISCUSSION QUESTIONS

I've come to realize that without reciprocity—give and take, pull and tug—there is little movement and growth. As such, what follows are questions for discussion. The Greeks believe that only through constant dialogue and honest sharing can friends reach a higher level of truth. Use these questions as jumping off points for your own conversations, and may we all keep learning and growing together.

<u>Growing Up, Finally</u>

- ➤ Do you feel you've grown up?

- ➤ Do you think age has merit? Does it matter how old you are in terms of your wisdom?

- ➤ Do you see yourself as an elder? What does elder mean to you? What personifies your ideal elder?

- ➤ Do you turn away from the word *crone* or embrace it?

You Don't Get a Gold Watch for Menopause

➤ Change is inevitable. Do you fight it or embrace it?

➤ What changes have been thrust upon you in the past five years, and how have you processed them?

➤ Would you welcome a ritual with friends to honor your achievements? What would you celebrate?

➤ Contemplate what transitions you have experienced in the past year and how well (or not) you've handled the challenges that come with change.

The Camera Never Blinks

➤ How much do you consider the effects your gene pool has had on the way you've managed your life?

➤ Are ancestors important to you? If so, why and who?

➤ What role should living relatives have in your life?

➤ What qualities are in your gene pool that can rise up and be there when the event seems too large for you to handle by yourself?

Figure Faults

➤ Do you like or detest your body?

➤ What does your body mean to you…a sacred vessel or a beautiful shell?

- ➤ How has your body served you?
- ➤ How can women work toward acceptance of their bodies even though they are not model perfect?

Time to Clean Out the Closet

- ➤ As we grow and change, so does our persona. Who do you represent now that you weren't a few years back?
- ➤ How comfortable would you be to dress your part instead of what is expected in your community?
- ➤ Would being an original free or embarrass you?

Rebel With a Cause

- ➤ How many rules have you broken lately?
- ➤ What does the word rebel mean to you?
- ➤ Is it time to be a rebel, or is it not appropriate for a grown woman?
- ➤ Wild and salty is how I see me…what words would you use to describe yourself?

Esteeming the Self

- ➤ Who are the people that compliment you? What do they say?
- ➤ From whom do you want the most appreciation and notice?
- ➤ How can you praise the gifts you have and give thanks for who you are, rather than holding on to old tapes that denigrate your being?

Multitasking No More

➤ A pause now and again is essential to being present in your day? How often do you slow down, and what activities allow you to BE?

➤ What aspects of life do you rush through? Can you squeeze more life out of certain events?

Scenes From a Very, Very Long Marriage

➤ Can knowing that to relate is a verb activate your partnership?

➤ Is long-term marriage outdated or worth it?

➤ If married, how did you survive functional relationship…that time when you were working hard for the very existence of the family? Or how are you surviving it?

➤ If your marriage came with a renewable contract, what would be in it?

What's Sex Got to Do With It?

➤ How important is sex in a long-term marriage?

➤ Is all the hype about erectile dysfunction and "being ready" natural, or is it a ploy by advertisers to make us believe we can go on having sex forever?

➤ What role does sensuality have in making your marriage intimate?

➤ Would you be satisfied with your relationship if it had only one of the following aspects: sexuality, sensuality, or intimacy?

Loving Unconditionally

- ➤ Are you a conditional lover?

- ➤ Who do you know or remember that loved you unconditionally?

- ➤ Do you try to steer clear of family members who love with conditions?

- ➤ Recall a time when you loved with no conditions. How can you apply that experience to someone you care about today?

Marital Marathon

- ➤ When you train for a race or begin a diet, there are rules to follow and a need to stick to a daily regimen. Such an agenda requires an overwhelming focus to get to the end result. Would such a focus make your relationship more meaningful?

- ➤ How can you activate your marriage?

- ➤ When running an ultramarathon everyone needs a team. Who is on your team when you need emotional and spiritual support?

Ripping the Velcro

- ➤ How can a mother prepare to let go of controlling her child?

- ➤ How can a parent stay involved but not invasive?

- ➤ When does motherhood end?

- ➤ Do you overrate your importance in your family's lives? What part of your role is outlived?

The Other Woman

- ➢ Why do you think there are mother-in-law jokes? Are you in that category?

- ➢ What frustrates you about being an in-law?

- ➢ Did you lose your son or daughter to their spouse?

- ➢ What are some ways to change this conundrum?

The Children Are Getting a Divorce

- ➢ When change is thrust upon you, how do you react?

- ➢ Can parents make a difference in their grown children's decisions?

- ➢ How can we learn to let go?

- ➢ What is the danger of obsessing?

- ➢ Discuss a situation where you worked your way through Elisabeth Kübler Ross's five stages of grief.

The Truth Is Rarely Spoken Because the Time Is Never Right

- ➢ How much do you crave real time with your grown children? Do you get it?

- ➢ What is the fear when communicating with your grown children?

- ➢ How do you keep judgment out of the equation and just celebrate who they are?

The Game Changer

> ➤ How could you make small changes that would ease tensions?

> ➤ What rules have you changed that have made a difference in your lifestyle?

> ➤ How could you let go of a job, relationship, duty, or event? How would that alleviate some of the chaos in your life?

Sign Language

> ➤ It's reasonable for everyone to dream. What might be a dream of yours?

> ➤ Do dreams have to be huge and amazing, or can you be as satisfied with small dreams? What would they be?

> ➤ When was the last time a dream or vision came to fruition in your life?

There's No Compensation for an Unlived Life

> ➤ Are you waiting for all your obligations to be finished before you take a plunge?

> ➤ Do you believe in carpe diem (seize the day)? Or do you feel your circumstances make it hard to achieve?

> ➤ When was the last time you dared to do something out of the ordinary?

> ➤ What do you recall were last year's meaningful events? Were you an active participant?

> ➤ How can taking time to receive a serendipitous moment make a difference in the living of a day?

ACKNOWLEDGEMENTS

It takes teamwork for a book to come to life. That has certainly been the case with *Stretch Marks*. Without the constant encouragement of colleague and friend Mary Anne Smrz, this book would never have happened. She navigated me through the entire process with her production capabilities and valuable contacts. A great debt is owed to "Scout" who went beyond the call of duty. Not only she, but the rest of the "fabulous four" all pitched in. Colleen Thomas and Dee Beckmann read and critiqued the material, while Ann Moss conceived and designed a concept that brought unity to this collection of essays. With her unique eye to both the "typewriter" face and layout she was able to connect my myriad thoughts from cover to cover. Laura Goodenow's editorial contribution was priceless—her ideas and sharp pen combined with her ability to understand my voice made working with her a dream. Her counsel, questions, comments and suggestions all made a significant contribution to this writer's creativity.

Early on, neighbor and friend Pam Beaubien edited many of the essays, always asking insightful questions that made them grow and expand from small thoughts to larger opinions. My faithful assistant, Cathy Stollen, worked night and day on every aspect of production and, as usual, offered counsel when needed. Heartfelt thanks to the patience Georgiann Baldino had throughout the fine tuning process, graphic changes, and knowledge of navigating through the tricky waters of publishing. And, finally, the encouragement and feedback from Vicki Armitage and Ann Glenn White was and is always appreciated, as are the responses from all the unfinished women readers who write to me about our common experiences.

About the Cover Art: Years ago when my writing career was in its infancy, my husband bought me this lithograph by Gretchen Dow Simpson at the Metropolitan Museum of Art. Titled Block Island, it was obviously a rendering of a woman bearing her soul on a typewriter. The framed original hangs over my desk to inspire continued stories. My gratitude to Gretchen for granting permission to use this important piece.

Gratitude and thanks to all!

Joan Anderson

ABOUT THE AUTHOR

Joan Anderson is an author, motivational speaker, and unfinished woman who hosts retreats for other unfinished women in search of themselves throughout the United States and in Iona, Scotland.

Her first memoir, *A Year by the Sea,* was on the *New York Times* Best Seller list for 32 weeks, followed by four additional books translated worldwide: *An Unfinished Marriage, A Walk on the Beach, A Weekend to Change Your Life,* and *The Second Journey.* Dubbed "the runaway wife," she has appeared on *Oprah, Weekend Today, Good Morning America,* and others.

Joan is also the author of 17 children's books and a magazine journalist. Her non-fiction book, *Breaking the TV Habit,* was the forerunner of "No-TV" week in schools throughout the country. She lives in Cape Cod with her husband.

www.joanandersononline.com
capewoman@msn.com

Notes to Myself

Notes to Myself

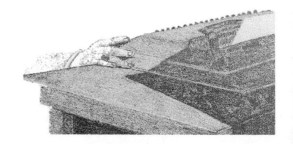

Notes to Myself

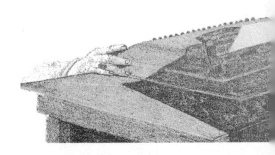

Notes to Myself

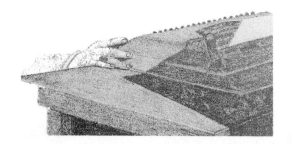

Notes to Myself

Notes to Myself